"My friend Dan Haight has written a masterful book which gives us powerful, practical keys concerning the harvest of God in our lives. You'll learn revelatory insights for how to live a more productive, bountiful life with an increasingly progressive harvest! Victory does not come in a day; it comes daily"

(Bishop Dale Carnegie Bronner, author and Senior Pastor of Word of Faith Family Worship Cathedral, Atlanta, Georgia).

"Pastor Danny Haight's integrity and straightforward approach to the Word of God are as refreshing as his insights are. It is God's desire for us to know and understand His will for our lives, and Pastor Danny helps us expand and unfold this truth. God makes known His ways in that He abundantly gives us wisdom and insight into His will. Pastor Danny Haight uses the Parable of the Sower (Mark 4) as the key which will give us insight into living the life of grace and faith. If we can understand this parable, we can understand all the parables. This book will inspire its readers to discover God's will for their individual lives, and I would therefore recommend Pastor Danny Haight's book, *Keys to Maximizing Your Harvest.*

(Pastor Ray McCauley, Senior Pastor, Rhema Bible Church, South Africa).

"God's Word is a storehouse of blessing and is our guide to a journey of purpose and success. Yet many people travel through life, never unlocking this treasure of wisdom and provision. In his compelling and insightful new book, Daniel Haight provides keys to understanding Scripture, helping people personally discover the power of God's Word for daily living. I encourage you to read this book, unlock the gift, and spend your days blessed by the treasure you find"

(Dr. Dave Martin, America's #1 Christian Success Coach and author of Twelve Traits of the Greats).

"Keys have only one intended purpose—to unlock something and to gain entrance. However, have you ever stood at a door trying to find the right key to fit that particular lock? In Keys to Maximizing Your Harvest, Daniel Haight will lead you to identify the key to assuring that the hearts of people are unlocked and Jesus can have entrance. Reaching people has just been made easier to understand and implement by the book you now hold in your hand. You're holding the Key"

(Dr. Samuel R. Chand, author of Cracking Your Church's Culture Code.)

"With inspirational stories, light-hearted humor, and wise insight, Pastor Dan Haight communicates tried and true biblical principles that have transformed the lives of thousands of people and can change your life, too. The scriptural truths found on the pages of *Keys to Maximizing Your Harvest* work. They work for people of all backgrounds, stages of life, and in every situation and circumstance. Apply these teachings, and they will work in amazing ways for you!"

(John Wagner, Lead Pastor, Turning Point Community Church, Lubbock, Texas).

"Great stuff! Christ's Parable of the Sower like you've never read it before! Time-tested principles that will heal the wounds of your past and walk you step by step into the future you have always longed for."

(Bob Gass, author and Bible teacher).

"Pastor Dan, we are excited about your new book, *Keys to Maximizing Your Harvest*. As you explain the Parable of the Sower, we know lives will be changed. God has blessed you with the wonderful gift of making His Word come alive"

(Pastor John Esposito, Christian Faith Center, Bloomfield, New Jersey).

"I have known Pastor Dan Haight for over twenty-six years. Not only does he possess a great insight into this critical parable, but Pastor Dan's life has demonstrated the successful practical application of the principles contained in the Parable of the Sower. In his book he reveals these principles in such a way that anyone can understand them and practice them so that they can live life as Jesus intended: life and life more abundantly"
(Pastor James Petrow, House on The Rock Family Church, Wind Gap, PA).

"My longtime friend Pastor Dan Haight tells it like it is, yet uses practical insight and humor that allows every reader to walk away with truths that will enhance their walk with the Lord"
(Pastor Joe McKelvey, Senior Pastor and Founder of Christian Faith Fellowship Family Church in Middletown, New York).

"Jesus said in Matthew 16:19 that He would give us the keys to the Kingdom of Heaven. Pastor Dan Haight gives you the master key that will open up doors of opportunity unlocking success and prosperity in every area of your life. *Keys to Maximizing Your Harvest* is a must read for every believer, and it will bring cycles of frustration to an end. Pastor Dan has laid out a blueprint that enables you to navigate from seedtime to the ultimate fulfillment of the abundant life, your harvest. Your days of feeling weary are over; read on and discover the key to experiencing your due season!"
(John Antonucci, Pastor, Faith Fellowship World Outreach Ministries).

"*Keys to Maximizing Your Harvest* is a must read for any believer who desires to deepen their walk with God and experience His abundance in every area of life. Pastor Daniel applies his keen biblical insight to a familiar parable to highlight major keys in the teaching of Jesus. This combined

with many great personal stories and relevant illustrations makes it a book that will encourage, challenge, and equip the reader to move to a new level of living"
(Lara Martin, UK worship leader and songwriter).

I have known Pastor Haight for over 25 years. We have served together on staff of a great church in New Jersey, have ministered together on missions trips and conferences, and I have had the great pleasure of ministering for him in his church. I am blessed to call him my friend. I can safely say that this book is an expression of how he lives his life both personally and professionally. Jesus is his example, and he wears Jesus well. I recommend that you read and meditate on the truths within the pages of this book. It will help you maintain the proper mindset and encourage you in your walk with God.

(Dr. Michael Landsman, Dean/Academic Head, Rhema Bible College, South Africa).

KEYS

to MAXIMIZING *your*

HARVEST

• • • • • • • • • • •

The PARABLE
of the SOWER

• • • • • • • • • • •

KEYS

to MAXIMIZING *your*

HARVEST

• • • • • • • • • • •

The PARABLE
of the SOWER

• • • • • • • • • • •

DANIEL J. HAIGHT

Bridge-Logos

Alachua, Florida 32615

Bridge-Logos

Alachua, FL 32615 USA

Keys To Maximizing Your Harvest
by Dan Haight

Printed in the United States of America.

Library of Congress Catalog Card Number: 2012952213
International Standard Book Number: 978-0-88270-894-2

Scripture quotations are from the NKJV: New King James Version of the Bible and the AMP: The Amplified Bible Version of the Bible.

CH 12-17-12

Dedication

This book is dedicated to the ones that sacrificed the most while writing this book: My wife Joselyn, she's my best friend and cheerleader, with whom I am proud to share my life with. My four children: Dominic, Emily, Chrissy, and David, I love you all. It's also dedicated to those who are seeking and hungering after righteousness.

Table of Contents

Foreword

I have known Pastor Dan for many years, both having faithfully served as a staff pastor for me, and as a successful and loyal pastor under my mentorship. He also serves as an Apostolic Team Leader for Covenant Ministries International, and is recognized by his peers as a true seasoned minister of The Gospel with experience and wisdom.

Ever since I have known him he has displayed an excitement for The Word of God, and has shown both integrity and tenacity to live It in his personal, family, and ministry life. His insight into the simple and practical approach to teaching and preaching has been penned in this book, that surely will serve to not only bless the reader, but to inspire and instruct them as well. Both his knowledge of The Word as well as his life experiences, are invaluable to building faith in the reader. I have been blessed to know him and call him a true spiritual son.

Congratulations to you Danny, your book is destined to touch many lives.

Dr. David T. Demola
Pastor, Faith Fellowship Ministries World Outreach Center,
President, Covenant Ministries International

Introduction
How the World Works
According to Jesus

The Bible we all read and study is not just a book! It is the inspired Word of God. It is the book that has the answer to life's questions and dilemmas that have baffled mankind. People say you never know what God's going to do. I want to challenge that thinking. If you don't know God's Word then I agree that you don't know what God's going to do. But, if you study His Word, you can't help but know He will do what He said He'd do.

I think we all get confused at times about God's timing but we shouldn't be confused about what He will do. I like what Dr. I.V. Hilliard says, "God is not mysterious. You can't write 66 books and tell people exactly what you're going to do and still be considered mysterious."

In late 1979 I began to focus on the Word of God with diligence. The Bible became everything to me. My personal life was in a free-fall so I became focused on God and His Word to survive! I took the Scripture Matthew 6:33 to heart. I started seeking God's Kingdom and it began to mean something important to me. I sought God with my whole heart. I took the Word at face value, what it said I believed and focused my attention on it. I began discovering that the Word was life and health according to Psalm 103:1-3. I took hours each night after work and concentrated on Scriptures in John chapters 14, 15, and 16.

All day on my job, as I performed my duties, I meditated on these Scriptures. I focused on believing there was life in the Word. Even though my personal life was in a free fall, I was so focused on God and His Word, that I hardly noticed it. I would confess over and over again the truth in the Word.

3

I would personalize all these Scriptures and confess them! John 14:21, *"He who has My commandments and keeps them, it is he who loves Me. And he who loves Me will be loved by My Father, and I will love him and manifest Myself to him."*

I was at work one day for a company that installed new power poles in Denver. It was just a typical day like all the others and we were working outdoors on the south side of Denver. I walked away from the group of guys I was working with to make sure the aluminum power lines that were going to be collected and wound into huge spools, were cleared of any debris. As I was walking hundreds of yards away from my co-workers, John 14:21, which I had been meditating on, came alive and Jesus appeared to me...He was walking next to me...He never turned toward me or spoke to me as we walked along...I just saw Him as we took several steps together.

In retrospect, I was at total ease walking next to the Lord. It couldn't have been more than a few moments. It was comfortable, peaceful and awesome. As soon as Jesus disappeared, I heard Him say, "No matter who else does in life, I will never leave you nor forsake you!"

You can imagine the mental and emotional calisthenics I went through trying to put this experience into its proper place as a young believer. I was trying to put it all in perspective. After all, who was I that Jesus would appear to me? I kept it to myself for the most part. I told a relative who thought I'd lost it, so I made it a point not to share it!

Something incredible happened through this experience. My expectation, sensitivity and awareness of spiritual things increased. I had spent time all those months meditating on the Word of God. And I saw the Word manifest. The curtain of the Spirit realm had been pulled back. I not only had the written Word of God to validate this supernatural experience, but I saw it first hand. It changed my life and heightened my expectations. Those who penned the Bible were people just like you and me, in all walks of life. They experienced the supernatural realm in their life. It says of the Apostle John in Revelation 1, while exiled and imprisoned on the Isle of Patmos, that he was in the spirit on The Lord's Day. John wasn't shocked or uncomfortable about his experience. We read about the spiritual realm throughout the Scripture. Meditation and concentration is how we increase our ability to discern God's ways. Nobody can do it for you.

This book is testimony to the power and ability of God to perform His Word. God wants us to live in the supernatural. We've limped through life long enough! The Lord told us He would lead us and guide us so our lives would be examples of a supernatural God as a sign and wonder to the unbelievers. John 16:13, *"However, when He, the Spirit of truth, has come, He will **guide you** into all truth; for He will not speak on His own authority, but whatever He hears He will speak; and He will tell **you** things to come."* [Bold emphasis added.]

I will share with you some of these supernatural interventions and how they correlate to the Word of God in all our lives along with the key. Jesus made a very important statement in Mark 4:13, *"He said to them, "Do you not understand this parable? How then will you understand all the parables?"* The key focuses on "this parable." In fact, this parable will help you understand the rest of them.

If there is a key to health, financial prosperity, and abundant life would you want to know it? If there is hidden truth that would unlock doors of opportunity, would you pursue it? In the Parable of the Sower, Jesus taught His closest followers that there were keys that would unlock knowledge so it would become understanding, and that this knowledge is not hidden from us, but for us.

And He said to them, 'To you has been entrusted the mystery of the kingdom of God [that is, the secret counsels of God which are hidden from the ungodly;]' (Mark 4:11

Amplified Bible)

Once we understand this, a whole new revelation can open for us. Mark 4:33 reads, *And with many such parables He spoke the Word to them as they were able to hear it. But without a parable He did not speak to them. And when they were alone, He explained all things to His disciples.*

Jesus used illustrations alongside the truth to give us understanding. It has been said that a pound of illustration is worth a ton of explanation. So, the stories we were given by the Lord were truths set alongside parables so that we could understand them.

We all have keys; keys to our office, home, car, motorcycle, RV, boat and snowmobile (though not here in Florida!). There are keys we have on our key rings that we have no idea what they are for. It's rather frustrating to try and open a locked door with the wrong key. I was walking through the church building recently without my master set when I came upon a locked door. I had to go all the way back to my office for the key. It's the same in life. Too many of us are locked out of our abundant lives that God has purchased for us, because of a lack of knowledge and understanding (Hosea 4:6-7). We know it is available, but we just can't seem to get the door open. We see victory and abundance in others but it remains elusive to many.

I want us to take a look at one key in particular in the Book of Mark. This is where Jesus said *"if you don't understand this....how then will you understand any..."* That sounds like an important point to me! We'll see the Parable of the Sower in (Mark chapter 4, Matthew chapter 13 and Luke chapter 8). We'll see the key that will unlock spiritual truth in every area of life. It will unlock truths that will catapult you into the place you've dreamed about. We have all dreamt about a great life, a happy home, and physical and financial stability. We've hoped for a place of emotional strength that will see us through every time.

I have good news! Jesus told us about the importance of a particular key. It too is hidden for us, not from us. We all like stories with mystery and suspense. Well, in Mark 4:11-12, the Bible teaches of hidden knowledge that is waiting to be discovered. Anyone can find it, but it's hidden for the diligent, persistent, and the hungry at heart.

Are you ready to start your search for the key to everything? Jesus taught His disciples using parables and examples of His day. A parable is a story about everyday life. Agriculture was something that was tied to every vocation of that time so everyone was familiar with the examples Jesus used. You may have to stretch your mind a little and think like a farmer so that you can understand. It will be plain to see, and it's right there under the surface waiting to be discovered.

Let's "till the fallow ground" in our hearts and learn together! It's waiting inside; a story to be discovered. Jesus used a great illustration that will open up all the other parables.

I trust when you read this book you will see the simplicity of the teachings of Jesus and how the Word of God works. This parable will explain the deceptions Satan uses to separate you from God's Word and into negativity. Galatians 6:9 says, *"And let us not grow weary while doing good, for in due season we shall reap if we do not lose heart."* (NKJV and Amplified)

Please note that the key bullets are topics to ponder as you read and will be marked by a key icon. 🔑

Also, all Scripture will be in the New King James version of the Bible unless stated otherwise.

Chapter 1
The Root Affects the Fruit

"Do you not understand this parable?
How then will you understand all the parables?"
Mark 4:13

As an example of how the things that seem small and insignificant and even hidden from view can affect everything, consider the following story:

The Curtain Rods

She spent the first day packing her belongings into boxes, crates and suitcases. On the second day, she had the movers come and collect her things.

On the third day, she sat down for the last time at their beautiful dining room table by candle light, put on some soft background music and feasted on a pound of shrimp, a jar of caviar and a bottle of Chardonnay.

When she had finished, she went into each and every room and deposited a few half-eaten shrimp dipped in caviar, into the hollow of the curtain rods. She then cleaned up the kitchen and left.

When the husband returned with his new girlfriend, all was bliss for the first few days. Then slowly, the house began to smell. They tried everything cleaning, mopping and airing the place out.

Vents were checked for dead rodents and carpets were steam cleaned. Air fresheners were hung everywhere. Exterminators were brought in to set off gas canisters, during which they had to move out for a few days, and in the end they even paid to replace the expensive wool carpeting. Nothing worked. People stopped coming over to visit. Repairmen refused to work in the house. The maid quit.

Finally, they could not take the stench any longer and decided to move. A month later, even though they had cut their price in half, they could not find a buyer for their stinky house. Word got out and eventually even the local Realtors refused to return their calls.

Finally, they had to borrow a huge sum of money from the bank to purchase a new place.

The ex-wife called the man and asked how things were going. He told her the saga of the rotting house. She listened politely and said that she missed her old home terribly, and would be willing to reduce her divorce settlement in exchange for getting the house back.

Knowing his ex-wife had no idea how bad the smell was, he agreed on a price that was about 1/10th of what the house had been worth, but only if she were to sign the papers that very day. She agreed and within the hour his lawyers delivered the paperwork.

A week later the man and his girlfriend stood smiling as they watched the moving company pack everything to take to their new home...including the curtain rods!

As a pastor, I see well meaning people try to change everything about their life overnight. I'm talking about changing the results of a lifetime of bad choices, and bad decisions overnight. If you want to start making huge changes, that's all well and good. Look at it this way: if you wanted to turn around an ocean liner, even in a storm, you'd be able to do it. However, it will take time, and you will have to make really wide turns allowing for many corrections, and a great length of time to do it. Life is like that. It all starts with making the first move, and that is sowing the right seed. Every tree starts with a seed. Its first job is to develop an adequate root system that will sustain that tree's growth and stability. Conquering yourself is the place to begin conquering life's problems. It all starts with a seed.

Are you full of fear? Well, you're going to have to sow a

seed that will bring you peace! Jesus is the Prince of Peace. The Word of God promises us peace, so the first place to start is filling up with the Word of God about the subject of peace. Plant a seed of peace by learning what true peace is. Get yourself some good resources to search through the Word of God. Find Bible verses to support where you need strength and change. Read, meditate, and think about the verses you studied. Speak them out loud. Let the seed of the Word of God grow deep down into the soil of your heart so a root system can develop and you'll stand through any storm or conquer any mountain.

🔑 It's the start that stops most of us!

We read about faith that can move mountains in: Mark 11:22-24,

> So Jesus answered and said to them, "Have faith in God. For assuredly, I say to you, whoever says to this mountain, 'Be removed and be cast into the sea,' and does not doubt in his heart, but believes that those things he says will be done, he will have whatever he says, Therefore I say to you, whatever things you ask when you pray, believe that you receive them, and you will have them."

A mountain is anything in your life that looks impossible to change, or to move. That's a great place to get to, but every trip starts with a first step! And the place to start is with the heart. You'll move mountains in life, but the heart is the place to start the process. How do we start the process of moving mountains? I'm glad you asked. As I said, it all starts with a seed. The Amplified translation of Proverbs 4:23 says, "Keep and guard your heart with all vigilance and above all that you guard, for out of it flow the springs of life."

Now when the Bible talks about the heart, it is not referring to the physical blood pump in your body. The heart is the core of a person. It is your spirit, which is alive to God,

11

and it also encompasses your soul which contains your mind, will, emotions, understanding, imagination and intellect. Guard your heart. 'Guard' is a military word. It is similar to the word that God used when He instructed Adam about his duties in the Garden of Eden in Genesis 2:15: *"And the Lord God took the man and put him in the Garden of Eden to tend and guard and keep it."* (Amplified Bible)

✐ If the garden needed to be protected, then there must have been an enemy to protect it from!

Your heart is where the Word of God is sown; your heart is the "soil." It must be protected and cultivated if you expect to "get a good crop". Keep and guard your heart, for out of it flows the issues (or boundaries) of life. The Hebrew word for "issues" is fountain. Remember Proverbs 4:23! What a powerful statement! Out of your heart flows life like a fountain. You live life from the heart. In the Living Bible, Proverbs 4:23 reads as follows:

"Guard your affections, for they influence everything else in your life."

In other words, whatever is in your heart influences how you see and perceive the issues of your life.

Ephesians 3:20 tells us that your heart is where the power source resides. Let's look at the parable of the sower; stay with me, it's a bit of a read, Mark 4:3-9,

"Listen! Behold, a sower went out to sow. And it happened, as he sowed, that some seed fell by the wayside; and the birds of the air came and devoured it. Some fell on stony ground, where it did not have much earth; and immediately it sprang up because it had no depth of earth. But when the sun was up it was scorched, and because it had no root it withered away. And some seed fell among thorns; and the thorns grew up and choked it, and it yielded no crop. But other seed fell on good ground and yielded a

crop that sprang up, increased and produced: some thirtyfold, some sixty, and some a hundred." And He said to them, "He who has ears to hear, let him hear!"

Jesus is speaking a parable to a multitude about seed and soil. The disciples, Jesus' disciplined followers, had a hard time understanding this so they asked for explanation. Let's look at Mark 4:13-14, *And He said to them, "Do you not understand this parable? How then will you understand all the parables? The sower sows the word."*

And verse 15 in the Amplified version,

"The ones along the path are those who have the Word sown [in their hearts], but when they hear, Satan comes at once and [by force] takes away the message which is sown in them."

If you don't have a healthy root of the Word growing in your heart, negative circumstances will cause you to stumble. You will get offended and start asking questions like "Why is this happening to me?" "Why is this so hard?" or "Why is this prayer not getting answered?" The Bible speaks of a root of bitterness in Hebrews 12:15; *"Looking carefully lest anyone fall short of the grace of God; lest any root of bitterness springing up cause trouble, and by this many become defiled."* A root is below the ground. You don't see it, but it becomes evident because it affects the life and the future of the plant and fruit. Healthy root, healthy fruit. Have you ever known someone who just exploded over nothing? Road rage for example; one minute everything is fine and the next, Boom! There's something growing inside; a root of bitterness and it affects the fruit.

🗝 There can be roots deep in the heart that can affect how we act and react to the issues of life. The roots affect the fruit.

Let me explain: If you don't guard your heart early in life, you can carry the criticism and negativity you experienced right into your future. Maybe you grew up in poverty and didn't have the benefits other children had. Children can be cruel. Many of us were teased and made fun of because we didn't have the benefits and advantages others were blessed with. These experiences can leave emotional scars that later can grow into a root of bitterness. You can live the rest of your life trying to impress people you don't know, spending money you don't have, buying things you don't need. Or, gathering possessions, expensive clothes, or jewelry all because of cruel comments made by someone in your past who just didn't know any better.

I have a pastor friend who always wore an old pair of shoes. They had worn out years before, but for some reason, he just kept on wearing them. Joselyn and I really care for him and for his wife, so we met them on a short vacation on the west coast of Florida. Now I knew he had enough money for new shoes, but I wondered why he kept and wore the old ones. When we were alone, I asked him why he kept wearing those old, worn out shoes. He said, "My dad died when I was young, and nobody ever taught me about the value of looking professional and dressing for success. I never really felt like I deserved nice things." It really touched me. I reminded him about who he is in Christ and told him that I'd teach him how to look like the professional he is. He took his life to a whole new level. It went from his shoes and clothes to every area of his life.

There are adults still trying to prove their parents' wrong years after their folks have died. Or maybe you've had a divorce, or someone cheated on you or abused you and told you no one would love or want you. So you live your life either hiding or trying to prove they were wrong. Words produce pictures in your mind. If they grow roots, you'll act or react to those words because of your perception.

Do you have a root of bitterness that is affecting your fruit daily? The root is below the surface of the ground, out of sight and mind, just like the shrimp in the curtain rod story. Just because something is out of sight, it does not make it insignificant. Are you seeing how important guarding your heart really is? You must protect yourself from negative emotions and experiences, because it is going to influence everything else in life. Think about that word: in-flu-ence. The flu is contagious.

🔑 Don't let a root of bitterness cause you to be influenced in a negative way.

It is not enough to uproot the bitterness that affects how you perceive life. You can also proactively avoid ever accepting that root by rejecting it.

If you get a knock on the front door and look out to see the FedEx or UPS delivery person standing there, you know they've got a package for you to sign for and receive. But what if the outside of the box was marked: 'Danger, Poisonous Rattlesnakes. Open With Extreme Caution?' As you stood in the doorway, with the box at your feet, you heard rattles coming from the box. What would you do? Most of us would say, 'I never ordered any rattlesnakes, I won't accept the delivery!' You can begin to proactively reject any influences that will harm or wound your future like words, thoughts or influences that are contrary to God's will.

The prescription for never getting a root of bitterness is right here in Proverbs 4:20-22, "*My son, give attention to my words; Incline your ear to my sayings. Do not let them depart from your eyes; Keep them in the midst of your heart. For they are life to those who find them, and health to all their flesh.* Get rooted in God. God has a plan for your life. "*As you therefore have received Christ Jesus the Lord, so walk in Him, rooted and built up in Him and established in the faith, as you have been taught, abounding in it with thanksgiving,*" (Colossians 2:6-7).

🔑 Attend!

Webster's Dictionary defines *attend* as 'to take care of, to minister, to serve, to listen and heed." So according to verses 20 to 22 in Proverbs 4, we are to take care of God's Word, to give attention to, to listen and to heed God's Word. So if a root of bitterness comes into my heart, I start attending to God's Word. I avoid a root by focusing on more important things. Once we get into this, you'll see how important it is to keep your root system healthy. We must think about what we think about.

🔑 Attending to God's Word means you focus on it. Whatever you focus on causes you to have a desire for it.

(Colossians 3:2 NKJV and Amplified) says to *"Set your minds on things above, not on things on the earth."* One translation says to, *"Set your affections on things above and not the things of this earth."* Attention affects your desires *"Let the word of Christ dwell in you richly in all wisdom, teaching and admonishing one another in psalms and hymns and spiritual songs, singing with grace in your hearts to the Lord."* (Colossians 3:16) Do you see a theme here? God expects you to attend to His Word and incline your ears to His sayings. (Proverbs 4:20) Webster defines *incline* as 'to have a tendency or preference.' Wow! To keep your heart with all diligence so that you can have the right issues flowing, just attend and incline! Always have a tendency and preference towards God's Word.

I've worked hard at keeping the Word as a preference. I've set up my life and the environment around me so it's easy to hear the Word! Whether its books that are readily accessible or teaching series on CD and digital formats, I've placed them in places I know I'll need them.

🔑 Focus is everything. Light focused becomes a laser.

Light is strong, powerful, and able to accomplish great deeds when it becomes focused. If your heart is focused on God's Word, and you're attending to His Word and inclining to His sayings, you'll be the powerhouse you've dreamed about becoming.

Proverbs 4:21 continues on to say, *"Do not let them (God's Words) depart from your eyes; Keep them in the midst of your heart."* You are encouraged to have the Word of God as your top priority, keeping it before your eyes and meditating on it in your heart. Jesus put it this way in (Mark 4:24 NKJV and Amplified), *Then He said to them, "Take heed what you hear. With the same measure you use, it will be measured to you; and to you who hear, more will be given. For whoever has, to him more will be given."* Be careful what you hear and see. Why? It all goes back to where you put your affections. Whatever you put your attention and affection on; you'll have a desire for.

⚷ Your eyes and ears are the gateway to your soul.

We think in pictures, and we reason in storylines—usually from the past. That's why we see behavior repeated over and over again. A person might be going along fine—sober, working hard and seemingly in control. But we are all products of our past experiences, and what we consistently do or repeatedly think about matters. Under pressure, this seemingly in control person might suddenly relapse into addiction. On the outside everything may seem great, but what are you seeing and thinking on the inside?

Proverbs 23:7 says, *"For as a man thinks in his heart, so is he."* What is the internal storyline playing over and over again in your recall? Undisciplined or immature people choose old thoughts and storylines to replay over and over in their minds. The super achievers in life choose their thoughts and storylines and play them on the canvas of their imagination. It takes work and discipline to proactively think productive thoughts.

Jesus was on His way to the Cross. His small group of followers had been told fourteen times of His upcoming crucifixion and resurrection. I'm sure they were anxious about the future. Jesus, knowing what the disciples would experience soon when they faced His crucifixion, gave them insight into weathering any storm. John 14:1-3,

"Let not your heart be troubled; you believe in God, believe also in Me. In My Father's house are many mansions; if it were not so, I would have told you. I go to prepare a place for you. And if I go and prepare a place for you, I will come again and receive you to Myself; that where I am, there you may be also."

Your heart is where you internalize, speculate and imagine. Much of what we face today can't compare with what the disciples faced, and Jesus talked to them about the condition of their hearts. Troubles in your heart can kill your seed or choke it to death. Remember, guard your heart with all diligence for out of it flow the issues of life.

Let's look at the story of David versus Goliath. The Bible says that David ran toward the giant Goliath.

Then David said to Saul, "Let no man's heart fail because of him; your servant will go and fight with this Philistine." And Saul said to David, "You are not able to go against this Philistine to fight with him; for you are a youth, and he a man of war from his youth." But David said to Saul, "Your servant used to keep his father's sheep, and when a lion or a bear came and took a lamb out of the flock, I went out after it and struck it, and delivered the lamb from its mouth; and when it arose against me, I caught it by its beard, and struck and killed it. Your servant has killed both lion and bear; and this uncircumcised

Philistine will be like one of them, seeing he has defied the armies of the living God...." *So it was, when the Philistine arose and came and drew near to meet David, that David hurried and ran toward the army to meet the Philistine.* (1 Samuel 17:32-36, 48)

David said, "I killed a lion and a bear." He chose to see himself killing the giant as he had the lion and the bear. That's what super achievers do in life. They see themselves winning beforehand. David chose correctly.

Do you have a dream, goal or God-given destiny? Use your imagination as a tool like David did to see your victory before the fight ever begins. (Ephesians 4:17 and 18 Amplified).

Today you can choose to renew your mind and expectations like most super achievers in life. They involve their imagination to visualize past victories and future ones. David said, "I recall my experiences with the lion and the bear and this giant will be like them." David already saw himself with victory over the giant!

Imagination is a tool to use as part of our arsenal to ensure victory in life. Today you can be like David and choose to use your imagination to work for you—not against you. Most people use this principle in reverse. They imagine all negative things happening to them. If you replay negatives and defeats over and over in your mind, you will be defeated. It's a biblical principle.

Job chose his own thoughts and chose incorrectly. Job 1:5 and 3:25 spoke of the things he feared: *"For the thing I greatly feared has come upon me, and what I dreaded has happened to me. I am not at ease, nor am I quiet; I have no rest, yet trouble comes."*

When it came to Abraham's time of testing and God told him to sacrifice his only son in Genesis 22:5, Abraham told his servants to wait for him, *"The lad and I will go yonder and worship, and we will come back to you."* He expected to return with his son completely whole. The negative reasoning or storylines Job played over and over again became his reality and so did the positive ones David and Abraham rehearsed. You can start to change today. Think about what you *think* about.

For years before I became a Christian, I would think and say negative things. I would curse my future with my thoughts and words. I would say things like, "Another day another dollar in debt." Ridiculous! Each year it seemed as if my life was getting more and more out of control.

Proverbs 23:7 puts it this way, *"For as he thinks in his heart, so is he."* Proverbs 18:21 tells us that *"Death and life are in the power of the tongue; and those who love it will eat its fruit.*

> ✐ **I had to change the storylines in my mind. I had to get the negative root out of my heart.**

Today I say what God says about me. Deuteronomy 28:6 tells me that *"Blessed shall you be as you come in, and blessed shall you be when you go out."* Ephesians 1:3 says that I have been blessed with *"every spiritual blessing in the heavenly places in Christ."* And 1 John 4:4 promises that *"He who is in you is greater than he who is in the world."*

Proverbs 4:22 says God's Word is, *"...life to those who find them and health to all their flesh."* So if we attend and incline, if we study the Word and meditate on it, we will have life and health. The Hebrew word for life means 'real life' or 'absolute life.' In other words, if we will attend to God's Word, listen to and understand His sayings, and keep and guard them in our hearts, we will have absolute, real life in us. Until we get serious about God's agenda, we haven't started living yet! Let's look and see what the Bible says about this: Proverbs 4:4, *"Let your heart retain My words; keep My commands, and live. Proverbs 2:7, He is a shield to those who walk uprightly."*

It's easy to see why you have to guard your heart, because the root affects the fruit. It's easy to see the importance of getting wisdom and understanding. To have that super abundant life you dream about, you must keep any roots of bitterness out of your heart, because that's where the fruit is produced, deep down in the roots. In the next several chapters, we talk in depth about the Parable of the Sower.

Any good farmer who desires a bumper crop always prepares the soil beforehand. A "bumper crop" is the maximum or premium yield. It's above and beyond an average crop return. A farmer must make sure he has all the tools, equipment and materials in good operating order. All the plows, disks, drills, irrigation, tractors, combines, barns, seeds, silos—everything must be ready to achieve optimum results. The farmer must be prepared for any conditions and situations that can and will arise. If you have ever lived on a farm, you know farmers are very helpful people. They are willing to lend a hand to a neighbor in need. During your process of growth and development, you're going to need help from a lot of people; your spouse, your pastor, teachers, friends, books, CD's, pod casts and downloads of messages. And when you see others struggling, help them as you've been helped!

There is a key to understanding life and how the Word operates in life. Jesus taught this principle in agricultural terms. Again life during this time was dependent on agriculture and farming. Most of the vocations of the day were tied or related to it in some way, and everyone knew something about it. That's why Jesus taught using these examples, so that everyone could understand. Today we're not as familiar with how things run on the farm. We're all pretty much removed from it. So let's start thinking like a farmer and prepare for a harvest.

Chapter 2
The Divine Order of God

*Then God said, "Let us make man in Our image,
according to Our likeness; let them have dominion over
the fish of the sea, over the birds of the air, and over the
cattle, over all the earth and over every creeping thing
that creeps on the earth. So God created man in His own
image; in the image of God He created him; male and
female He created them. Then God blessed them, and God
said to them, "Be fruitful and multiply; fill the earth and
subdue it; have dominion over the fish of the sea, over the
birds of the air, and over every living thing that moves on
the earth." Genesis 1:26-28*

We're created in the image and likeness of God and God
is our example. God spoke and things changed. It says in
Genesis 1:2 that, *the earth was without form, and void;...*
The Hebrew words without form means chaos. The Earth
was in chaos until God spoke. Genesis 1:3 records that He
simply said, "Let there be light"; and there was light. To bring
order to chaos, He spoke!

⚷ The divine order for man, who is created in the image and likeness of God, is to dominate his circumstances as God does.

God speaks words and things change! Things go from
chaos to order. We know there's a spiritual realm because the
Bible tells us there is. (See Colossians 1:16.) We are spirit,
we have a soul, and we live in a body. The Bible states that
God is Spirit and that we must worship Him in spirit and in
truth (See John 4:24.). We impact this natural realm with our
words which have an effect in the unseen realm.

🔑 God designed man to impact the natural from the supernatural.

So how do we do that? How do we impact this natural realm with our words? We do that by believing and speaking. That's what faith is, we believe something in our hearts, and then we say what we believe. Faith is our response to what God has already said. Now that may seem radical to you, but we believe and speak everyday! The difference is that we gather sensory information from the world around us. The car makes a funny noise, "Oh no! My brakes must be going; I'll need to get them fixed." We don't know for certain it's the brakes, but because of sensory information we've gathered, we believe something, and we speak! Well here's the difference in the Kingdom of God. We take spiritual information, we read in the Word of God, 1 Peter 2:24, "by His stripes we were healed..." We sneeze, "A-choo!" Instead of saying "I must be catching a cold," We believe what God has already said concerning our health and we say, "By His stripes we are healed in Jesus name!" We believe God's Word over the circumstances and sensory realm information. We believe and we speak.

In Acts 3:6 the Apostle *Peter said, "Silver and gold I do not have, but what I do have I give you: In the name of Jesus Christ of Nazareth, rise up and walk."*

God's Word carries life, power and authority. When we're speaking God's Word, it is meant to carry power and authority too.

The seed in the Parable of the Sower is the Word of God. Look at the power that's built into the Word. Psalm 19:7 says, *"The law of the Lord is perfect converting [restoring] the soul: The testimony of the Lord is sure making wise the simple."* This teaches us that the seed of the Word can restore our souls. Man has the ability to impact this natural realm with the power of the living Word. In other words, our authority comes from God's power delegated to man to make an impact here on Earth! We can move our "mountains," that is, problems with the Word of God.

There is a divine order of God. The divine order includes man speaking God's Word. Words have the power of life or death in them (See Proverbs 18:21.). Words are seeds that go and create an atmosphere and platform for miracles and the will of God to be established. Words are seeds. And, there are many other types of seed also. Everything God has given you is a potential seed that can produce a harvest.

In the natural, seeds are made to be planted in soil, germinate and grow. The supernatural side to sowing and reaping is a concept God established. There is life built into the Word. John 1:1-4 states that Jesus is the Word personified. *"In Him was Life…"* The divine order of God is for man to take the Word and change his circumstances.

The seed has the power to produce and the potential to become a plant and bear fruit. When God made oranges, He created them so they produced seeds while they also produce fruit.

You impact this natural realm by not only understanding that there is a supernatural realm, but by cooperating with the principles which ensure optimum return. Colossians 1:16 teaches us that there were things created that are in Heaven (the spirit realm) and things created that are on Earth (the natural realm). It also teaches that there are things invisible and visible.

God gave mankind dominion and authority, the right to govern and control their lives (See Genesis 1:26.). We have a responsibility to stand up spiritually and work with the system. We have a part to play in that and I learned it the hard way.

᧞ God designed man to impact the natural from the supernatural

I was invited to go out fishing in the Gulf of Mexico with

a nationally known minister. The night before we were to go fishing, I had a supernatural dream. The Lord was trying to warn us not to go out fishing. There were going to be engine problems and a storm, and God was trying to lead us from that unseen realm and affect the seen realm. The dream was vivid and accurate. My dream was, we were out fishing and the sky got dark and the wind started blowing. Waves started crashing over the boat, almost like the opening scene in Gilligan's Island; and in the distance the grim reaper was walking across the top of the water, sickle in hand to take us. I woke up startled. I went back to sleep and got up early to go on that boat, not mentioning anything about the dream to my wife or the guys on the boat.

It was to be an all day trip of about 20 miles from the shore. It took a good hour and a half to get out to the reef to fish. You'll never guess what happened. "The weather started getting rough, the tiny ship was tossed. If not for the courage of the fearless crew, the minnow would be lost..." Sorry! That was the theme from Gilligan's Island. Anyway, the sky got dark, the wind began to blow, waves came up and we started to have engine trouble. One engine was emitting carbon monoxide and it was affecting all of us. Two or three guys passed out and I was going in and out of consciousness. We limped the 20 miles back to shore with one bad engine and we all almost died because I didn't respond to the supernatural realm. God tried to warn us and show us what was to come through my dream. (See Acts 2:17.) One facet of our arsenal is dreams and visions. These are just a few of the ways we can cooperate with the divine order of God and affect the natural from the supernatural. I'm so glad the story had a good ending, but we could have avoided the drama. We could have postponed the trip, had the boat checked out. We could have gone out another time and had a wonderful trip.

God loves man and wants to help us if we will let Him. We have to be a doer not just a hearer of the Word (See

James 1:22-25.). It could mean life or death if we ignore God's leading.

God has an order, and we must respect that order if we're going to get the results we read about in the Bible. God not only created man in His image and likeness and gave him authority on this Earth, but God also gave man the ability to dominate this world system by using the seedtime and harvest principle and authority to dominate and control our lives (See Genesis 1:26-28.). Genesis 8:22 tells us, *"While the earth remains, seedtime and harvest, cold and heat, winter and summer, and day and night shall not cease."* If you follow God's order, you'll become effective when it comes to seedtime and harvest. If an optimum return is possible, then I want to realize it and live it! So in order to optimize, we must follow God's order.

The will of God is not automatic. If it was, then most of the Bible is superfluous. One of the biggest lies told is the one that comes from many pulpits stating, if it's God's will, it will automatically happen. We have to think and not check our brains at the church door. If that is true then why aren't all people saved? (See 2 Peter 3:9, and 1 Timothy 2:24.) After all, it's His will that all be saved and come to the knowledge of the truth. Are all coming to the knowledge of the truth? No, I see people who haven't grown spiritually in decades. Why? Because the will of God is not automatic, it must be sought, contended for and desired with one's whole heart (See Jeremiah 29:13.). Mankind, God's creation, has the right to govern and control our lives. We've been given dominion and authority because there is an enemy to contend with!

You need accurate information about what your rights and privileges are in the Kingdom of God. Look at it this way, my wife took her car in for repair. One of her car door locks was malfunctioning and would not unlock. As she sat with her service repair advisor, he asked if the car had an extended warranty since it had over 50,000 miles. "I don't know." She replied. Fortunately he found information that stated her car was certified and had an extended warranty to 100,000 miles. This saved us a pretty penny! It would have been an expensive repair. She was unaware of the rights and privileges associated with her certified vehicle. So too, many believers are unaware of the extended warranty (our covenant) associated with the Word of God. It's our job to know!

The animal and plant worlds are not sustained by seedtime and harvest in the sense that man is. God just takes care of them as stated in Matthew 6:26-30. *"Look at the birds of the air, for they neither sow nor reap nor gather into barns; yet your heavenly Father feeds them. Are you not of more value than they?"* God called mankind to live by the law of seedtime and harvest. What are we talking about here? God gave us seedtime and harvest principles so that by implementing them, we could potentially obtain a great, best possible, maximum harvest. The quality of the harvest depends on what you do!

Take an oak tree. During the life of an oak, it produces a multitude of acorns. But during its whole life, which may span decades, its natural harvest may only be one or two acorns that will take root and grow up as oaks beside the parent tree. Now there are many reasons why only a few acorns will produce. Deer, squirrels, hogs and other animals eat the acorns. The "ground" under the great oak hasn't been prepared for planting. Insects and weather have an effect on the acorns.

🗝 The greatest reason why there's such a small natural harvest is because man is not involved in the process.

God instituted seedtime and harvest. If you introduce man into the process of growing oak trees, watch out! Man is part of the divine order of God.

My former Associate Pastor, Jonathan Ables, bought his

first automobile by harvesting acorns. Jonathan didn't take the acorns and plant them; he sold them to tree farmers. Amazing! The seed of the oak tree produced many times over: financially for Jonathan when he gathered and sold them; and again for the farmers when they planted, grew and sold the trees. One acorn produced over and over again once man got involved. Jonathan harvested thousands of sacks over the years, and each sack held hundreds of acorns. Because man has been called by God to follow the laws of seedtime and harvest, we have progressed from one oak tree's acorns producing one or two mature trees over the lifetime to that same tree having every acorn produce a mature tree. This is all because God called man to get involved in the process. Once man is involved in the seedtime and harvest process, he can optimize the process. Man's involvement is the key to the divine order of God.

We need to get the revelation that our future harvests are in our hands in seed form. When someone who is called by God controls their seed properly, harvest is on the way. It's only the farmers who plant and manage their seed that can expect the harvest.

I recently taped a TV broadcast for our weekly television program. I had a businessman and minister friend of mine on as a guest. He stated that one of his relatives had just recently come back to the Lord and rededicated their life. They began implementing the principles of God's Word. They started making right decisions and sowing good seed. It was amazing how quickly the Lord began to restore their life which included their relationships, job, finances and favor. Restoration was evident. I said, "It's amazing how a few good decisions can put us in position to reap good results." One sign of maturity is when we start taking responsibility for our choices. This young person got things right with God and His favor, seed time and harvest began to produce good results.

Are you in a place where you need restoration and God's

help? Mankind has the divine order of God at its disposal. Think about it, God left authority in man's hand and made a covenant with him.

🔑 **Today you're just a few good decisions away from having God's best working with you and for you. Choose to follow God's process.**

"I call heaven and earth as witnesses today against you, that I have set before you life and death, blessing and cursing; therefore choose life…" That's in Deuteronomy chapter 30 starting at verse 19.

Now let's review: seedtime and harvest is not just for acorns, tomatoes or finances. Begin to sow forgiveness and understanding. Begin by being nice. Sow seeds of friendship and unity and watch how life begins to change.

🔑 **God has called you and me to impact this world with His divine order.**

You are created in the image and likeness of God, and you have the authority to sow seed and reap a harvest. You get to determine the quality of that harvest! Speak God's Word in every situation for His Word out of your mouth is God's divine order.

Chapter 3
Four Keys to the Harvest
Key Number 1—The Seed

"While the earth remains, seedtime and harvest, cold and heat, winter and summer, and day and night shall not cease." Genesis 8:22

The parable of the sower is recorded in 3 Gospels, Matthew 13, Mark 4 and Luke 8. All three writers give us different aspects and valuable information in order for us to walk in these truths of God's divine order.

I love how Dr. Luke gets right to the point in verse 11. The seed is the Word of God. No ambiguity there. God's not hiding anything from us. This mystery is not being hidden from us but for us. To anyone who is seeking for truth there is another standard.

And He said to them, "To you has been entrusted the mystery of the kingdom of God [that is the secret counsels of God which are hidden from the ungodly]; but for those outside [of our circle] everything becomes a parable, In order that they may [indeed] look and look but not see and perceive, and may hear and hear but not grasp and comprehend, lest haply they should turn again, and it [their willful rejection of the truth] should be forgiven them (Mark 4:11-12 Amplified)."

The seed is the Word. Let me introduce something here we will cover in more depth later on. Answers to all of life's questions are covered in the Word.

"Grace and peace be multiplied to you in the knowledge of God and of Jesus our Lord, as His divine power has given to us all things that pertain

*to life and godliness, through the knowledge of Him
who called us by glory and virtue, by which have been
given to us exceedingly great and precious promises,
that through these you may be partakers of the divine
nature, having escaped the corruption that is in the
world through lust. But also for this very reason,
giving all diligence, add to your faith virtue, to virtue
knowledge, to knowledge self-control, to self-control
perseverance, to perseverance godliness, to godliness
brotherly kindness, and to brotherly kindness love.
For if these things are yours and abound, you will
be neither barren nor unfruitful in the knowledge of
our Lord Jesus Christ. For he who lacks these things
is shortsighted, even to blindness, and has forgotten
that he was cleansed from his old sins. Therefore,
brethren, be even more diligent to make your call
and election sure, for if you do these things you will
never stumble;"* (2 Peter 1:2-10).

The seed to the harvest of any problem you have in life is
found in the Word. The Bible has an opinion about everything
you're faced with; from who you should marry to who you
should vote for, to how much tax you should pay and what
you should do with your time, talent, tithe and attention.
You can go to the Word for anything and if you seek, you
will find (See Matthew 6:33.).

God has an opinion about our lives because He wants our
lives to be abundant (See John 10:10.). The only way for an
abundant life to be secured is for us to seek God's Word as we
would silver and gold (Proverbs 4:13-18, Proverbs 8:34-35,
Psalm 19:7). The Word of God is perfect, restoring our souls
to their original condition. Every one of us has had our mind
and emotions affected in life; some of us by abuse, divorce,
neglect or some self-inflicted act. This is a hard cold world
and it can rock you and affect you in ways that can hinder
you for the rest of your life, time doesn't heal all wounds,

only the law of the Lord is perfect in restoring our souls to their original condition (See Psalm 19:7).

We've all heard testimony in church or on TV of what some people have had to go through. Once they allow God's Word to convert or restore their souls, they're back to their original condition. Only the Word, the seed can do that. There are probably some areas of life that contain burdens you have been carrying around. Year after year they are still there. Only you can let the Word restore you. It takes a seed, a seed with life in it, to restore your soul. The seed is one of the keys to your harvest. Let's look at four main keys to every harvest.

There are four keys to the harvest that we are going to be covering in the next few chapters. Let's begin with the first key: The Seed. God placed the seedtime and harvest principle in the same category as cold and heat, summer and winter, and day and night.

🗝 Cold and heat, summer and winter are as consistent and dependable as the sun rising and setting and the seasons changing.

God has associated seedtime and harvest in the same way. Whether or not you want it to be cold or hot, light or dark; it is a certainty that you will experience these variables. And in the same way, whether or not you *want* to experience the inevitability of seedtime and harvest, you will. You can't stop heat and cold, you can't stop light and darkness, and you can't stop the seasons. All you can do is prepare and adjust to them because they are the law.

You will reap what you have sown in this life.

"Do not be deceived and deluded and misled: God will not allow Himself to be sneered at (scorned, disdained, or mocked by mere pretensions, or by His precepts being set aside). [He inevitably deludes himself who attempts to delude God.] For whatever a man sows, that and only that is what he will reap"

(Galatians 6:7 Amplified Bible).

There's no way around this fact. By the authority of God's Word, your good intentions don't change things. Our feelings, family traditions, chills, goose bumps, or hair standing up on the back of our necks don't move God. Only what you sow in this life dictates the harvest, and you should always consider what you're sowing. If you sow corn seeds, you'll reap more corn. If you sow watermelons, you'll reap more watermelons. Every farmer knows they'll reap whatever seed they put into the ground.

Have you ever met people who have drama and problems all the time? We all have. If you examine their lives, you'll see that they have a habit of sowing drama in every area of life—family, finances, friends, and work. Having continual strife and drama becomes a habit, drama can be addicting for some. It's a reaping of seed sown. Galatians 6:7 says, *"Do not be deceived, God is not mocked; for whatever a man sows, that he will also reap."*

A habit of strife, gossip and dissatisfaction always results in a harvest of the same. There's no getting around it, you are a product of seeds sown. Do you want a better, healthier, wealthier, saner, more peaceful harvest next reaping season? Then sow the requisite seed. The New Living Translation, Galatians 6:7 reads, *"Do not be misled—you cannot mock the justice of God. You will always harvest what you plant."* A man's harvest in life is a result of his seed.

As a pastor, I've heard lots of stories. Many of them start with the same sentences: "I never saw it coming," or "How did this happen to me?" I've started some of my own stories with the same sentences. But once we take the time to examine all the seeds sown to bring us to that point, we usually find out that our words and our actions played the biggest part of our reaping. Proverbs 18:21 tells us *that "Death and life are in the power of the tongue; those who use it must reap the fruit it yields."* Words and actions are seeds sown that produce harvests. For many years, I have said that those who say they can and those who say they can't are both right.

Seed always produces after its own kind. If you want to start changing drama and strife, start changing your seed. Start by being nice. Compliment people; don't correct them all the time. Make a quality decision not to have an opinion about everything. It's a liberating day when you realize that you're not the only person God has available to change the world. Start your day by trying to compliment loved ones. Start your day by being optimistic about your prospects. Begin by thanking God for your house or apartment, for your family and friends, your job or business. Someone once said if we would be more thoughtful we would be more thankful. Start saying what God says about your opportunities and relationships. Pretty soon your words of encouragement will spring up into a harvest of peace and contentment. If you have an old beat up car, don't curse it, bless it! "Car, you're old and worn out, but you'll keep running until I can afford to upgrade."

With your positive scriptural words working as seeds for your future, you'll see a change for the better. What's more, people will see a change in you and begin to like you and bless your life.

Haven't we all had to work at being positive from time to time? With the world being so negative, it's easy to fall into the flow of negativism. That's why study time in the Bible and positive influences as far as music, radio and TV are so important. We should all strive to be more optimistic, expecting God's best in life.

⚿ I've never seen a happy mean person, have you?

Let your attitude reflect a new you, sowing seeds of encouragement to people all around you. Your life can't help but increase with favor and opportunity. Solomon teaches us in Ecclesiastes 9:11,

> *"I returned and saw under the sun that the race is not to the swift, nor the battle to the strong, nor bread to the wise, nor riches to men of understanding, nor favor to men of skill, but time and chance happen to them all."*

About a year ago I was flying out of Newark airport to come back to Florida after preaching for a few days. So, I wanted a sip of a vanilla milk shake and I walked over to a concession stand in Terminal A. An employee, a young girl with a sour attitude, walked over and just scowled at me. Not with a cheerful, "Welcome to Mc'whatever, how may I help you?", but with a blank stare. I said hello to her and asked her for a small vanilla shake. She never said a word, just turned around and drew it out of the machine. I handed her a five dollar bill, and as she started to make change, I told her to keep the difference. Her whole countenance brightened up and she smiled. I said to her, "Are you kidding me? Are you going to allow a $2.50 tip to determine your attitude? Sweetheart, if you'll just smile and serve your customers with enthusiasm, I promise you, you'll get plenty of tips." That's just a scriptural law. What you sow, you reap. It will work anywhere you are, from Anchorage to Miami, Minneapolis or Micanopy. You reap what you sow. Here's an important point you don't want to miss:

⚷ Sow your best seed to reap your best harvest.

Any farmer or rancher will tell you about their commitment to the seed they use. Whether it's the seed for the crops of the field or the reproductive seed of the livestock, the farmer is always looking for the premium. They look for registered seed that has a history of great yields so they will produce a bumper crop, or they search through the bloodlines of bulls for the ones which will produce large healthy offspring. The seed must always be the best. How would you expect the best harvest without planting the best seed? You wouldn't but believers do it all the time. We've all met people who are just plain mean. If they would only adjust their attitudes and put a smile on their faces, it would change so much about their overall mindset.

Smiling alone makes you feel good and has the potential of sowing a positive seed wherever you go. We should get caught smiling and being happy, sowing a good seed. A simple smile releases endorphins into our bodies.

Farmers and ranchers, at least the ones that put forethought and resources into the best seed, expect with great anticipation that they will receive an exceptional crop. They can be optimistic because they know the potential of the seed, which has been pre-engineered. The future is built into its history, and each seed has a pedigree or track record. The farmer knows a lot about the future of the seed by knowing about its history. So the farmer knows that if he wants a bumper crop that will yield incredible return, he must use a seed that has great potential.

There is life in the seed. A funny thing about that seed, however, is that for it to produce more seed, it has to die first. Don't try and understand it. Your brain will hurt if you try and figure out the process. All farmers know the seed must die to live. They don't know exactly how it happens, but it doesn't stop them from working the process. In John 12:24 Jesus tells us, *"Most assuredly, I say to you, unless a grain of wheat falls into the ground and dies, it remains alone; but if it does, it produces much grain."* The ability to produce life and its ability to reproduce is already built into the seed.

The Word of God is filled with seeds of life. If you put the Word of God in your soul, you will reap the life that is in it. The way it works is amazing.

"This Book of the Law shall not depart from your mouth, but you shall meditate in it day and night, that

*you may observe to do according to all that is written
in it. For then you will make your way prosperous,
and then you will have good success."* (Joshua 1:8).

Dr. Roy Hicks says, "If you put the Word in you when
you don't need it, the Holy Spirit will remind you of it when
you do need it." If you keep feeding on the Word consistently,
there will be a transformation. We are promised that this is
true in the following Scriptures:

*"My son, give attention to my words; incline your
ear to my sayings. Do not let them depart from your
eyes; Keep them in the midst of your heart; For they
are life to those who find them, and health to all their
flesh."* (Proverbs 4:20-22)

*"For as the rain comes down, and the snow from
heaven, and do not return there, but water the earth,
and make it bring forth and bud, that it may give seed
to the sower and bread to the eater, so shall My word
be that goes forth from My mouth; it shall not return
to Me void, but it shall accomplish what I please,
and it shall prosper in the thing for which I sent it."*
Isaiah 55:10-11

*"But other seed fell on good ground and yielded
a crop that sprang up, increased and produced: some
thirty-fold, some sixty, and some a hundred."* (Mark 4:8)

These are a few passages that illustrate another law: there
is life in the Word. The seed of the Word of God is ultimate in
quality. There's nothing to compare to the absolute flawless
quality and ability of the Word of God. So as you proactively
apply the Word to your life, you anticipate an increasing
harvest of life; a harvest of favor, health, righteousness,
prosperity and joy.

✐ The Word is the ultimate seed every believer should be planting daily in the soil of the soul.

Books, teaching series, seminars, and services are all great, but there's no seed that can compare to actually reading and studying the Word of God yourself. Second Timothy 2:15 encourages us to study to show ourselves approved to God. Take the time everyday to read and study the Scripture, even if it's only a few minutes. It is how we get to know God, and how we learn how to have "good success", as it says in Joshua 1:8.

⚷ The seeds you sow in life will determine your future harvest.

Your future is completely dependent upon the seeds you sow now. As a matter of fact, you're reaping a harvest in life today because of the seeds sown in your past. Say "Amen" or "Oh me." Good seed or bad, that's the process under which you're working. This is the way Jesus said life works.

One night around dinner time, my wife said that she hadn't been sleeping well, eating properly, thinking proactively, or just taking care of herself in general, and that it was no wonder that she wasn't feeling well as a result. She told me she was going to go to bed earlier to get the proper rest. Wow! She was thinking about sowing the seeds of proper rest, so that the next day, she could be at her optimum.

I just read Bishop Dale Bronner this morning quoting Mark Twain. "...the only way to keep your health is to eat what you don't want, drink what you don't like, and do what you'd rather not." Mark Twain was just talking about sowing the right seed.

Are you completely satisfied with your life? There are so many facets to living, and they must all be ministered to. The bible covers everyday life, health, happiness, peace, joy, favor, relationships and finances, not just in the sweet by and by.

In my opinion, there are at least seven dominant areas of life that have to be sown into if we want to maximize our return:

1. Spiritual Life
2. Physical Body
3. Mental Life
4. Social Life
5. Financial Life
6. Emotional Life
7. Family Life

Solomon gives us interesting insight regarding these seven areas. Ecclesiastes 11:1-2 tell us to, *"Cast your bread upon the waters, for you will find it after many days. Give a serving to seven, and also to eight, for you do not know what evil will be on the earth."* He tells us to give a portion to seven and also to eight. Well, which one is it? I'd been taught that there are only seven main areas in life.

As I began to meditate on these thoughts, I recalled God's character. He created us as free moral beings with the right to choose, we are not mind numbed robots. God lays out our choices in Deuteronomy 30:19, *"I call heaven and earth as witnesses today against you, that I have set before you life and death, blessing and cursing; therefore, choose life, that both you and your descendants may live."* He sets before us blessing and cursing and encourages us to choose life. But we get to make the choice.

God's will is not automatic. That's why the Scripture tells us to choose blessings, choose life. Choose to sow your best seed.

God not only has an earthly plan, but an eternal plan, and has called us and commissioned us with the awesome responsibility of world outreach. I believe that is the eighth part: to choose to sow our lives as seed into reaching a lost, dying and crying world with the good news that Jesus paid the price of our sin, allowing us all to receive the gift of eternal life. John 3:16-17 tell us,

> *For God so loved the world that He gave His only begotten Son, that whoever believes in Him should*

not perish but have everlasting life. For God did not send His Son into the world to condemn the world, but that the world through Him might be saved.
After His resurrection, Jesus appeared to the disciples and gave them the Great Commission, ordering them in Mark 16:15-16, *"Go into all the world and preach the gospel to every creature. He who believes and is baptized will be saved; but he who does not believe will be condemned."* It's called the Great Commission, not the Great Suggestion. So if you're not satisfied with your life, start sowing your best seed into each of these eight dominant areas of life:

1. The Spiritual: Are you committed to God's plan for your spiritual life? Are you a disciple? Are you maturing? Are you involved in and submitted to a local church? Hebrews 10:25 warns us against, *"...forsaking the assembling of ourselves together, as is the manner of some, but exhorting one another, and so much the more as you see the Day approaching."*

In Matthew 6:33, Jesus told us to seek first the Kingdom! Webster defines Kingdom as: *a*: the eternal kingship of God *b*: the realm in which God's will is fulfilled. In Matthew 5:16 we are told to hunger and thirst after righteousness. Have you ever seen a truly hungry person eat? On TV they're feeding hungry children in some far off country. They mob the food – spilling much in their desperation. All rules of decorum and protocol go out the window. People who are hungry will eat almost anything.

The same is true for a person who is hungry spiritually. It seems like they can never get enough, always buying a new book or teaching series. A person who is hungry for food can satisfy their craving in just a few minutes. Someone who is hungry for God's Word is never satisfied. They are always hungry for more. Brother Kenneth E. Hagin put it this way, "The more you know, the more you're eligible to know; because the Bible is a progressive revelation."

You and I know people who got saved and never really grew from that day forward. Spiritual growth is not automatic. So here's the question. Why do some folks grow and others seem like they could care less? Growth takes work, discipline, consistency and focus.

"If then you were raised with Christ, seek those things which are above, where Christ is, sitting at the right hand of God. Set your mind on things above, not on things on the earth." (Colossians 3:1-2),

"As you therefore have received Christ Jesus the Lord, so walk in Him, rooted and built up in Him and established in the faith, as you have been taught, abounding in it with thanksgiving." (Colossians 2:6-7).

"Even when we were dead in trespasses, made us alive together with Christ (by grace you have been saved)," *"But now in Christ Jesus you who once were far off have been brought near by the blood of Christ.* (Ephesians 2:5, 2:13).

Someone once said the sign of maturity is when people start taking responsibility for their actions. Stop feeling sorry for yourself and take responsibility. Spiritual growth is a result of what you've been eating. If you're not hungry for God, taste and see that He is good and you'll want more. *"Oh, taste and see that the LORD is good; Blessed is the man who trusts in Him!"* (Psalm 34:8).

2. The Physical Body: God only gave us one body. You must sow proper nutrition, water, rest and exercise for optimum results. When the body is abused, ministry is over.

3. Mental Life: I hope you have chosen to be a lifelong learner. Statistics show that people who keep their minds stimulated live longer and healthier lives. It's a choice. I have a pastor friend who is always asking me, "Danny, what are you reading?" He once told me that there are three things which can change your future: the books you read, the people you associate with, and the seeds you sow. Be a lifelong learner.

Remember, today a reader, tomorrow a leader.

4. Social Life: As we discussed earlier, God made us three part beings: spirit, soul and body. You have a soul that has been created for interaction with others. Solitary confinement is a punishment for a reason. Social inactivity will restrict us in other areas, so we must develop good relationships (See Proverbs 18:24.). If you don't have any good friends, start by asking God for a friend and be friendly.

5. Financial Life: Ben Franklin once said, "Common sense isn't so common." There are plans and seminars everywhere to help in this area of life. If you don't have a plan, get one and be disciplined. I've heard it said, "If your outgo exceeds your income, then your upkeep will be your downfall." Have a plan. Be disciplined. I have taught the 70-10-10-10 principle for years in seminars and services. Live off 70% of your income, spend 10% of your income, save and invest 10% of your income, and tithe 10% of your income.

6. Emotional Life: You must have a plan for your emotional life, because everywhere you turn there's bad news. If it's not counterbalanced, bad news will have a cumulative effect on your soul. Philippians 2:5-6 out of the Amplified Bible encourages us to,

"Let this same attitude and purpose and [humble] mind be in you which was in Christ Jesus: [Let Him be your example in humility] who, although being essentially one with God and in the form of God [possessing the fullness of the attributes which made God God], did not think this equality was a thing to be eagerly grasped or retained."

Train yourself to be a humble well balanced person. One of the characteristics of people who are unbalanced emotionally is unrealistic expectations. We live in a broken world with dysfunctional people and our expectations should be in the Lord and His promises, not unstable people!

The seed of the Word will help balance us out emotionally

so we're not like a yoyo going up and down. God's Words have life in them and will build us emotionally. Let the mind that was in Christ Jesus be in you.

✒ We have a choice as to what we think about.

Pick and choose your thoughts, because they turn into emotions and actions and so on. 2 Corinthians 10:4-5 (Amplified Version) tells us,

"For the weapons of our warfare are not physical [weapons of flesh and blood], but they are mighty before God for the overthrow and destruction of strongholds, [inasmuch as we] refute arguments and theories and reasonings and every proud and lofty thing that sets itself up against the [true] knowledge of God; and we lead every thought and purpose away captive into the obedience of Christ (the Messiah, the Anointed One)."

The way of the world is a blue Monday, terrible Tuesday, weird Wednesday, almost Friday Thursday, Thank God it's Friday, and so on. Choose your thoughts wisely. There was a very humorous sign posted decades ago at the beginning of the Alaskan Highway. When it rained up there or the snow melted, the water got the dirt road all muddy and deep ruts and grooves wore into the muddy roads. The sign read, "Choose your rut wisely, you'll be in it for a while." Choose your thoughts wisely for they will turn into emotions, emotions into strongholds, strongholds into actions, actions into routines and routines into traditions. Your traditions turn into destiny.

7. **Family:** I heard someone say once that 90% of your joy and 90% of your aggravation will be a product of this one choice: whom you marry. You must choose to always sow your best seed into your family. Wives, sow encouragement, affection and attention into your husbands. Husbands, love your wife and learn what ministers to them: flowers, cards,

vacations, gifts, attention or (all of the above). The divorce rate among Christian marriages is comparable to those who don't believe in Christ, and that shouldn't be so.

I was recently in Orlando on vacation, and while I was there, I turned on the Trinity Broadcasting Network. Dr. Phil was on a show, talking about relationships. He explained that nearly half of all marriages end in divorce. He also mentioned that when couples pray together regularly, the divorce rate drops to 1 in 10,000. Let's sow our best seeds to our families and reap a great harvest.

8. **World Harvest:** Reaching lost people for Christ, and fulfilling the Great Commission takes effort, strategy and finances. Ask God to use you in the harvest. Ask God to use you to help others that are praying around the world for their loved ones that live in your city. Pray for your pastor to have a passion for reaching out to the lost and then help him to do so. Find a family this week and invite them to your church. Tell them you'll buy them lunch after service at their favorite restaurant. Scripture tells us that we should ask God for lost people.

"Go out into the highways and hedges, and compel them to come in, that my house may be filled." (Luke 14:23)

"The Lord is not slack concerning His promise, as some count slackness, but is longsuffering toward us, not willing that any should perish but that all should come to repentance." (2 Peter 3:9)

"Ask of Me, and I will give you the nations for your inheritance, and the ends of the earth for your possession." (Psalm 2:8)

Let's commit today to sow our best seed into each of these eight areas of life. If you want to reap a better harvest in life, it will take an intentional seed. As the farmer plants the best seed, the registered seed, so should you. Your harvest depends on it.

We all have seeds that we've planted long ago that are dormant now. You may have given up on them long ago. You may have even forgotten those dreams but there is still life there. Seeds have been found from decades ago, centuries ago. Seeds have even been found dormant in the pyramids. Once you plant those seeds even though they have been dormant for centuries they sprout and produce. Why? Because there is life in the seed. It's the same with the Word and the dreams in your heart. Let hope bring life back to your dreams. All you need is the light of the Word to bring them back to life. Remember you can do all things through Christ who strengthens you. Never forget that the gifts and callings of God are unchanging (See Romans 11:29.).

Chapter 4
Key Number 2—The Season

Don't despise the day of small beginnings!
(See Zechariah 4:10.)

There are different seasons in all of our lives. Right now I'm in a transitional season. It's erratic and not as predictable as other times. At different seasons in our lives, we need to prepare ourselves and our heart not to be distracted or discouraged. Once you plant your seed, from our perspective, it can seem like nothing is happening. If we could only see below the surface of the soil, we'd see there is a lot going on. It's slow going and gradual but much is happening. Understanding your season settles a lot of questions.

Not too long ago I was in one of those seasons. It didn't seem like much was going on above the surface of ground and I began to speculate and even worry about my future. During a trip to New Jersey from Florida, I flew in very early and made it to the hotel by 11:00 am. I had planned a day of relaxation and study as I would be speaking at my home church that evening. As I was checking into the hotel at the front desk, there seemed to be a loud commotion at the other end of the lobby. As I turned to see what the noise was, the lady at the front desk said, "Oh we have a convention of special needs teachers and administrators at the hotel this week. That man over there speaking loudly is their guest celebrity."

"Oh, who is it," I asked. She said "Have you ever seen the movie Rainman?"

"Yes," I said and she then told me, "That's Rainman, George Finn." He actually passed away last year. Anyway, I didn't think anymore about it and went up to my room.

I was struggling with the season I was in. I had all day to pray, study, and be alone. I wanted answers to what seemed like a dry season. Really when I got right down to it, I was fluctuating between the love of God and was God really concerned with little old me in a lonely hotel room. It took a while, but I got over my pity party. Once I started focusing on God and not my feelings, I got peace. (See Colossians 3:1, 23, Matthew 7:7, Matthew 12:35, and Psalm 40:1-2.) Isn't it wonderful the answers to all life's questions and problems are in the Word? I was anxious about the season I was in but about an hour or two later I was settled and had peace. (Isaiah 43:1-2) Just a little side note, this is a faith walk, God doesn't show us our entire life mission in an instant. If He did, it would scare us too much. Before I knew it, it was 6:00 pm and I was downstairs in the lobby waiting for my ride to take me to speak at the evening service at church.

Out of nowhere, Mr. Rainman came over and grabbed me and pulled my face about 2 or 3 inches from his face saying, "What's your name?" I answered, "Danny Haight," while at the same time I was trying to pull away from him. Lots of things were flashing in my mind. Why did he grab me? Why is he so close to me? Is Rainman going to kiss me or what? I really didn't know if I wanted that on my resume or not…"This just in, Rainman kisses Florida pastor in the lobby of a hotel, details at 9:00." Rainman said, "Danny, God has a special plan for your life. He's going to use you to help people with special needs." He asked me, "What do you do?" I said, "I'm a pastor of a church and all our people have special needs." He said, "Danny, where do you live? (Now remember, I'm 2 inches from his face and I've been trying to pull away during these nervous moments.)

I said I lived in Fort Myers Florida and that must have triggered something in him because he started singing the Simon and Garfunkel song, Mrs. Robinson. He let go of me with one arm and that's when I made my escape. He started to sing, "Where have you gone, Joe DiMaggio? Our nation turns its lonely eyes to you." Then all the people in the lobby said "woo woo, woo…" So I sang, "Coo, Coo, Ca-choo, Mrs. Robinson, Jesus loves you more than you will know wo, wo, wo…." This really happened.

About that time some folks from the special needs conference walked over and took control of Rainman. I tell this story to encourage you. You may be in a strange season right now in your life. Remember, if God needs to get you to another state to have a Rainman tell you that God has a special plan for your life, He will if that's what it takes.

What season are you in and how do you make the most of it? Doing your best today puts you in the best position for tomorrow.

There are four main keys to any harvest:
🗝 (1) the seed you plant,
🗝 (2) the soil you plant it in,
🗝 (3) the season you choose to plant in, and
🗝 (4) the servant who plants and maintains the crop.

You are in control of all four of these keys. You can choose wisely and get a great return or you can be unwise and haphazard and your yield will be poor at best. It will take a few chapters to learn about these four keys.

At the end of this chapter, we will learn about a fifth key. A *supernatural season*. This is God's domain. He dominates this season.

In this chapter we're covering seasons. All four keys are critical to a good harvest. If you only get one or two of these keys right, you'll probably starve. No farmer would ever buy the best seed and prepare the soil perfectly, and then not take the time of year into account. Ecclesiastes 3:1-3 & 11 tells us, *"To everything there is a season, a time for every purpose…."*

Remember, there is a season for everything. If you try to plow your fields too early in the spring and the soil is still soggy from the rain and melting snow of winter, you'll get your tractor stuck. But if you ignore the spring and summer and plow in December, the fields are frozen solid. God has given us natural laws and seasons so that we can optimize the seedtime and harvest principle. When it's spring, it's time to prepare the fields for the seed. Summer is growing season, when the rains will come to water the crops. Once fall arrives, it's time to harvest. If you wait too long to harvest your crop, the rain that once fed your crops will turn to hail and destroy all of your hard work. Natural laws and seasons are God given so we can use them to position ourselves for *repeated and predictable results*. That's why we follow recipes for cooking, why we follow maps or GPS's for traveling. That's why football teams practice all week.

✍ So we can get repeated and predictable results.

We can use natural law to our benefit. (See 1 Corinthians 11:1.) Paul said follow the Lord. Paul had learned some things he wanted to teach others so they didn't have to learn it on there own. Mistakes are costly and time consuming. By following a regimen of faith, we can have predictable maximum results.

There are times in life when you can practically and spiritually discern if it's plowing, sowing, watering or reaping season. Firstly, you already know that you can't reap a harvest if you haven't sown for one. You know logically that if the seed and season aren't right, you won't maximize your crop. You know spiritually that your harvest will come gradually *"For the earth yields crops by itself: first the blade, then the head, after that the full grain in the head. But when the grain ripens, immediately he puts in the sickle, because the harvest has come."* (Mark 4:28-29) So we know that if you're newly saved or maturing in the principles of God, you're not going to get a harvest the day after you plant. That is called a miracle and we're not in control of the timing or results of miracles. Miracles are suddenly and just enough to save you from catastrophe. God delivers with miracles. He sustains us with favor, the blessing of God on our lives and the law of seed time and harvest. (See Genesis 8:22.) Seed time and harvest are gradual and predictable. If you're new at the things of God, you need to understand that there's a process. So don't get discouraged if you sow in the evening and don't reap by morning. Galatians 6:9 tells us, *"And let us not grow weary while doing good, for in due season we shall reap if we do not lose heart."*

How many times in my spiritual immaturity did I get moved during a church service and give a large seed in an offering and expect the harvest the next morning. I didn't understand there is a process and there are seasons.

I have worked these principles for over twenty years of my life. Therefore, I am in a season where I should be getting better results when compared with the first few years of learning the process. Some people look at their lives today, and they think that God is arbitrary, that He blesses one and not the other. That's not true! Look deeper and understand that we're all in different seasons and different places of maturity. Don't get weary. Keep pressing on and expect great things. Depend on God's grace and be persistent. (See James1:4.) Allow patience to have its perfect work.

(See 2 Corinthians 10:12.) Don't fall into the trap of comparing yourself to others and where they are in their seasons. You don't know what they've sown. You weren't there when they prepared for their harvests. We can only control ourselves and our own actions. Don't think for one minute you know about other's lives. There's danger in comparing because it will just lead to speculation and trouble. (See James 3:16.) There are times in our lives that there will be hard work. They'll seem harder than other times. This is especially true if you're at the plowing and planting stages but looking impatiently to the harvest. Plowing and planting just aren't as fun as harvesting! But they're necessary. You'd better not try to skip any of the steps. When it comes to your future harvest, do what needs to be done in each season of the year and each season of life. If you have an argument with someone, don't let it go for ten to twenty years before you apologize. Take care of it in its season. (See Ephesians 4:26) Don't let the sun go down on your wrath. (See Mark 11:25.)While praying, go and forgive.

Remember that the time to give financial seed is all year long so when you have seed in your hand, plant it! Ecclesiastes 11:1 tells us to *"Cast your bread upon the waters, for you will find it after many days."* At least that's what you should do if you want a harvest all year long. But it is especially important to sow financial seed when you have a harvest and financial increase. During times of plenty, plant good seed for future harvests.

Luke 6:38, *"Give, and it will be given to you: good measure, pressed down, shaken together, and running over will be put into your bosom. For with the same measure that you use, it will be measured back to you."* Here's the real answer. When it comes to the season you are in and the season you want to be in next, you get to choose the measure that your next season will be. (Luke 6:38b) *"For with the same measure that you use, it will be measured back to you."*

If you want it to be a small season with small puny returns or harvest, then plant small puny seed. If you want a healthy large harvest, then choose your measure or amount wisely. If you sow with a thimble, that's how it will be measured back to you. If you sow by the truckload, that's the measure God uses to give back to you. That ought to answer about 90% of all your questions about your present harvest. Makes you think about sowing good large seed doesn't it?

🔑 **Just remember, if you wait for perfect conditions, you'll never sow your seed at all.**

Ecclesiastes 11:4 in the Amplified version reads, *"He who observes the wind [and waits for all conditions to be favorable] will not sow, and he who regards the clouds will not reap."* Don't we all know people who just can't pull the trigger on giving or forgiving? They have great ideas and intentions, but never sow that seed! This inability is the result of a hard heart. You've heard the old saying, 'Ready, aim, fire!' Well, lots of believers who want a great harvest in their future will hold their seed, waiting for just the right time. For them the saying should be, 'Ready, aim, aim, aim...' Galatians 6:7-9 teaches us, *"Do not be deceived, God is not mocked; for whatever a man sows, that he will also reap. For he who sows to his flesh will of the flesh reap corruption, but he who sows to the Spirit will of the Spirit reap everlasting life."* And let us not grow weary while doing good, for in due season we shall reap if we do not lose heart." These Scriptures should keep us right on target in identifying our season. We will reap what we sow. We can't miss whole sowing seasons and expect to reap a great harvest. Any practical farmer knows that.

I recently met with a man in his 70's who told me when he met his wife; she said she was a good Lutheran girl who believed in tithing. He said I knew I'd better become a tither too if I wanted to marry this girl. So he said that for 50 years, the first check he writes is to God.

Proverbs 29:18 reads, *"Where there is no revelation, the people cast off restraint; but happy is he who keeps the law."* If you don't have a prophetic revelation of the seedtime and harvest principle, you'll cast off restraint. You'll lose your focus, and the harvest will be lost. Hebrews 10:35-36 reminds us to endure,

> *"Therefore do not cast away your confidence, which has great reward. For you have need of endurance, so that after you have done the will of God, you may receive the promise."*

Your faith works; it's a gift from God (See Ephesians

2:8-9.) So don't get weary while doing good for in due season you will reap a harvest.

Be bold and have courage like God told Joshua (See Joshua 1:8.), you reap if you don't faint. In one of the most familiar faith Scriptures, Jesus told the disciples that even in the face of a mountain (problem); to speak to it, to believe and not to doubt in their hearts, and the mountain will move. (See Mark 11:22-24.)

Seasons are part of life. We must learn to cooperate with them. There is no mountain out there that is too big for you when you have the Word planted in your heart. The Word has life in it to move these mountains. We can listen to the devil's lies that this problem is the one that can't be fixed. That's a lie. Jesus said all power is given to me now you (disciples) go! (See Matthew 28:18-19.) Jesus gave us the keys to the Kingdom and that qualifies us for victory in any season.

"And I also say to you that you are Peter, and on this rock I will build My church, and the gates of Hades shall not prevail against it. And I will give you the keys of the kingdom of heaven, and whatever you bind on earth will be bound in heaven, and whatever you loose on earth will be loose in heaven." (Matthew 16:18-19)

"Then He called His twelve disciples together and gave them power and authority over all demons, and to cure diseases. He sent them to preach the kingdom of God and to heal the sick." (Luke 9:1-2)

"Then the seventy returned with joy, saying, "Lord, even the demons are subject to us in Your name." And He said to them, "I saw Satan fall like lightning from heaven. Behold, I give you the authority to trample on serpents and scorpions, and over all the power of the enemy, and nothing shall by any means hurt you. Nevertheless do not rejoice in this, that the spirits are subject to you, but rather

rejoice because your names are written in heaven."
(Luke 10:17-20)

We can't get caught up in unbelief no matter what season we're in! God's Word is truth not Satan's, and not our circumstances. Jesus had to rebuke Peter once for listening to the wrong voice. Even though moments before, Peter was the only disciple who had the revelation that Jesus was the Messiah. Peter boldly said, *"You are the Christ, the Son of the living God."* (Matthew 16:16-19). Then moments later Jesus rebukes Peter for being mindful of man and not God. (See Matthew 16:21-24.) Circumstances are what you see when you get your eyes off God's Word.

Wow, Peter went on some roller coaster ride that day. Peter confesses Jesus as Christ and moments later allows Satan to use him as a potential stumbling block against Jesus.

What season are you in? Peter didn't control his soul and his thoughts. Jesus has a remedy for that. (See Matthew 16:24-27.) Lay your life down. Follow God's ways and truth. Your seasons will be better and more productive! *"If you faint in the day of adversity, Your strength is small."* (Proverbs 24:10)

As you read this book, what season do you find yourself in? Are you plowing, sowing, fertilizing, reaping or preparing? Don't wad up your confidence and throw it away. 1 Timothy 6:12 tells us to, *"Fight the good fight of faith, lay hold on eternal life, to which you were also called and have confessed the good confession in the presence of many witnesses."* Keep fighting the good fight of faith, and you'll reap. As Romans 8:31 says, *"...what then shall we say to these things? If God is for us, who can be against us?"* God is for you! Follow His principles and your seasons will be fruitful.

Chapter 5
Key Number 3—The Soil

Any farmer that's worth his salt prepares the soil before planting time. Every step of the process of seed and soil preparation is done with the harvest in mind. Farmers prepare diligently with proven processes that have yielded great results year after year. They plow, dig, disk, and remove rocks and debris. They add fertilizer and irrigate the ground, preparing it with the harvest in mind.

🗝 The heart of man is represented by the soil in the Parable of the Sower.

"Listen! Behold, a sower went out to sow. And it happened, as he sowed, that some seed fell by the wayside; and the birds of the air came and devoured it. Some fell on stony ground, where it did not have much earth; and immediately it sprang up because it had no depth of earth. But when the sun was up it was scorched, and because it had no root, it withered away. And some seed fell among thorns; and the thorns grew up and choked it, and it yielded no crop. But other seed fell on good ground and yielded a crop that sprang up, increased and produced: some thirty-fold, some sixty, and some a hundred" (Mark 4:3-8).

The soil is an integral part in the process of growing an incredible crop, a step that cannot be ignored if the farmer is to maximize his or her opportunity for harvest. Neglecting the preparation of the ground could have catastrophic effects on the harvest, because each step of the process is important and will affect the outcome. Having a plan that works, a proven plan that has yielded crops time after time can ensure maximum results. I don't know about you, but I don't just want to go through the motions. I want results. And if a one

57

hundred fold return is available, I want to shoot for it. I'd rather shoot for one hundred fold and hit seventy five, than shoot for nothing and hit it every time.

When it comes to the soil of our hearts, we must prepare the ground in order to get everything out of our hearts that would be detrimental for spiritual growth. Strife, unforgiveness, sin, selfishness, fear and unbelief will all affect the ability of our hearts to be conducive for bearing fruit. In the upcoming chapters, this will be our main focus: preparing the soil of our hearts for optimum growth and development. Remember, the ground under the oak tree wasn't prepared to receive the acorn, and thousands of seeds rotted away before another oak tree was produced. We have to take care of the condition of our hearts so we can produce the kind of life and fruit we desire, in the right season.

Remember, Proverbs 23:4 says, *"Keep your heart with all diligence, for out of it springs the issues of life."* Our heart is the soil we plant in. That's why we must guard and protect it from hardness, stones, thistles and thorns. Jesus would take His disciples aside when the ministry was too draining or busy and instruct them to keep their hearts pure. Mark 6:30-32 tells us of such a time:

"Then the apostles gathered to Jesus and told Him all things, both what they had done and what they had taught. And He said to them, 'Come aside by yourselves to a deserted place and rest a while.' For there were many coming and going, and they did not even have time to eat. So they departed to a deserted place in the boat by themselves."

You can curse a whole season by being distracted by peripheral issues. Don't prolong your season with the condition of the soil of your heart with wrong seed. Your constant busyness is detrimental to a pure heart. (See Luke 10:39-42.) Martha was distracted by busyness and issues of no eternal significance. She missed the glorious being. You need time to stop, reflect, pray, and be quiet before God. Just like Jesus, we need time to be by ourselves and rest for awhile. Create seasons in your life to be with Jesus; to be in God presence. (See Genesis 2:2)

I heard Gloria Copeland talk about how she was going through a very difficult problem in ministry. She said she took time to read the Gospels and Book of Acts through four times that month in addition to her other studies. She went on to say that the additional focus on the Word brought a breakthrough. I did the same thing after I heard her and it created an atmosphere of faith in my life. (See Colossians 3:1-2.)

It's what gets in our hearts that blesses or curses us. We are what we think about. When computers were in their early stages, there was a saying, 'Garbage in, garbage out.' It's true in computers, and it's true in our hearts. You can only get out of it what you put into it. Guard your heart. Be aware of the season you're at in life. If you want to reap, you must sow into good ground.

There are four natural seasons; Winter, Spring, Summer and Fall. These seasons all have their advantages and purpose. There is another season, a 5th season and that is Due Season (See Galatians 6:9.) says due season always comes.

🔑 We block the Word of God out of our hearts by trying to plant the Word in hard ground.

In Mark 4:3-4, Jesus said, *"Listen! Behold, a sower went out to sow. And it happened as he sowed, that some seed fell by the wayside; and the birds of the air came and devoured it."*

I read the Bible for years before I became a Christian. I had it in my head somewhere that if I just read the Bible, then once I died, I could tell God, "Hey, I read your book!" and that would be my get out of jail card, pass go and collect $200 and get my free pass to Heaven. Sounds crazy, but

I really believed it. Even though I had a hard heart, I read the Bible year after year, all the while complaining that it was too difficult to understand. Later I learned it was only difficult because I wasn't born again and my heart was hard. The Word couldn't penetrate my hard heart anymore than a seed thrown into a field could penetrate crusty hardened ground.

I'm going to tell on myself here. Right before I truly got saved, I made a deal with God. I said, "Lord, I'm going to come home from work every day and read several chapters of your book." I figured once I read the Bible from cover to cover, that this constant conviction that wouldn't leave me alone would finally let up and just let me live my life. Well, three months later, after sitting in my chair reading every day, I finally finished the Bible. I didn't understand it. I hadn't stopped any of my partying and wild living, but at least I'd finished reading it. The next thing that happened really surprised me though. The following day when I came home from work, I picked up the Bible and started reading from the beginning again. "In the beginning, God created the heavens and the earth…" Another three months passed. I finished it again, and my heart was finally in a condition where I could receive the seed of salvation. My heart had softened up enough for the seed of salvation to take root.

I trusted Christ as my Savior and then all of a sudden, those passages started making sense. I'd found the key to the lock of eternal life. I was a changed man. The people around me thought I had lost my mind and thank God, I had. Isn't it funny that when I abused alcohol daily, experimented with drugs and had my priorities wrong, I was okay with most people. But when I read the Bible and lived it by giving, forgiving, being nicer, caring, helping, and contributing to society, I suddenly became a fanatic.

The Bible that was so hard to understand became progressively more understandable. Once the condition of my heart began to change, I started to understand the keys to the kingdom. Matthew 16:19 promises, *"I will give you the keys of the kingdom of heaven..."*

The first key was to get the revelation that Jesus took my place on Calvary's Cross. His spotless blood paid the price for sin, and I could accept the free gift of salvation by faith. And that, my friend, changed everything for me. As I studied more, I learned that salvation was the beginning, not the end, and that salvation was the first key to getting rid of the hard heart talked about in Mark chapter 4. My pastor said it 25 years ago. "I'm not trying to find out what I'm going to become some day." He said, "I'm trying to find out what I've already become."

Paul wrote in 2 Corinthians 5:17, *"Therefore, if anyone is in Christ, he is a new creation; old things have passed away; behold, all things have become new."* You became a new creature in Christ. A new species of being that never existed before. Ezekiel 11:19-20 reads,

"Then I will give them one heart, and I will put a new spirit within them, and take the stony heart out of their flesh, and give them a heart of flesh, that they may walk in My statutes and keep My judgments and do them; and they shall be My people, and I will be their God."

I want to tell you a supernatural story about what great lengths God will go to get the Word planted in a person's heart. As a pastor you come across a myriad of people from week to week. We had a family in the church that came regularly except the elderly husband. Periodically, when he'd attend, I race to the parking lot as soon as possible to say a few words to him when service ended. I always kept it light and jovial.

He would say, "Hey preacher, don't get used to me coming regularly. I just come once in a while to make sure my wife doesn't give you too much money." Truth be told, he didn't have to worry about is wife giving too much money.

One night I had a very vivid dream about this gentleman. I saw him laying in a coffin at his funeral. I also saw him walking to the altar and giving his life to Christ. I woke up in the morning and told my wife that he was going to die but that he was going to get saved first. My wife wondered whether we should tell him or the family. I said, "No, I don't think so. God started this. He will finish it." A funny thing happened that Wednesday night at service. This man and his whole family were in church. He never came to Wednesday evening service so I thought this is it. I taught the service, gave a salvation call and he never moved. Sunday rolled around and he and the whole family were there. I thought this is it. I taught and gave about three altar calls but again, he never moved. I was getting concerned now because I knew he was going to die. I wanted to help God by now. The next Wednesday night he came to service again. Since he had never been to three services in a six month period, and never three services in a row, I knew God was up to something. I taught, gave an altar call, gave another, nothing. I was about to close the service and asked, "Is there anyone here who just wants hands laid on them? His wife said from the back of the room, "My husband has been a little tired the last few days, please pray for him." He came forward and I laid hands on him, prayed the prayer of faith and just sat him down in the front row. I gave one more altar call and he reached up and gave me his hand and gave his heart to Christ.

That was Wednesday night. Saturday morning at 6:00 am got the call from his wife telling me that she had found he had died in his sleep. She then asked, "Do you think he really got saved?" I told her about the dream and she cried and cried and I cried too.

God loves people and will touch this realm from the spirit realm. He will put a new heart in someone. God gives us a new heart, one not made of stone, but of flesh. Now don't start singing "Que sera, sera., whatever will be will be..."

because that's not the truth.

I don't know about you but a lot of us had a lot of junk in our hearts. We hung around the wrong people and their dysfunction became acceptable. Maybe it was the way we were raised or our neighbors. As children, we allowed a lot of debris to get in the once fertile soil of our hearts. Divorce, strife, and drama all adds up to our hearts being affected. Being hard hearted is a condition that is not only contrary to growth, but will keep you frustrated your whole Christian life. That's why many people stop following Christ altogether or are chronic complainers about God and His ability to perform His Word.

You know people just like that. The hardness of their hearts has basically kept their lives in a perpetual holding pattern because the seed of the Word of God could never penetrate a hard heart. Therefore they are destined for spiritual mediocrity and frustration. A new heart must be maintained.

Soon after my salvation, I attended Bible School. My brother Mike was enrolled at a school in Broken Arrow, Oklahoma so I applied and was accepted. I worked at a restaurant in Tulsa where the bartender was a young man who was raised by his mom who was a well known local minister. One day, while placing my order for one of my tables, this young man, who was raised right but was living far from God, said to me in a sarcastic tone, "Praise God lay your hands on me young preacher and make this pounding headache go away." He was mocking me and he raised his hands in a joking manner. Before he knew it, I reached across the bar, put my hand on his head and commanded the pain in Jesus' name to free him. The power of God hit him right there and he said, "I'm healed, the pain is gone!" I told him that even when we're joking around, God takes us seriously. His heart began to be good ground that day.

Salvation affected me deeply! I've seen others you couldn't

tell much of a difference. I once saw flowers growing in front of an apartment building while I was driving down the road and I had to pull over to look at God's creation. They were beautiful and I stood there crying as I realized I had never noticed what God had done before. I had to pull over and look at God's creation. I was standing there crying that I had never noticed what God had done before! I believe one of the key ingredients to all of us keeping spiritually sensitive is to keep listening to the Word. (See Mark 4:23.) Keep a steady flow through your eyes and ears. (See Mark 4:24 NKJV and the Amplified Version.)

🔑 Although God has a plan for your life, it is not automatic.

Salvation is the starting line, not the finishing line. Mark 4:4 says, *"And it happened, as he sowed, that some seed fell by the wayside; and the birds of the air came and devoured it."* Some seed fell by the wayside could be better translated as fell on the path or road.

As you drive out to the country, you see farm after farm, and separating these farms are roads, and to each side of the road are swells or ditches. Some roads are paved, many are not. Farmers in Jesus' day sowed seed by throwing or slinging the seed into the field. That sort of sowing is called broadcasting. The farmer would throw a handful of seed in the direction of the tilled soil. Sure, there was somewhat of an art form to the broadcasting of seed, but you can understand how, when a farmer came to the edge of his field, some seed could be sown by accident on the road, the path, or the ditches.

🔑 To unlock the potential of the seed, it must go into fertile ground, not on top of a hard packed road.

To really get an understanding of this principle, picture a

farmer broadcasting seed by slinging handfuls into the field. Some seeds end up on the hard packed path or road, and the birds swoop down and just take the seed. (See Mark 4:4.)

No farmer would ever expect a crop to grow on top of a hard packed road, but Christians do it all the time. We listen to the Word of God being taught or we study the Word on our own, yet some never take the time to see that the ground is well tended to. No wonder few believers are experiencing "the land that is flowing with milk and honey (See Exodus 3:8.)" It's so easy for the birds of the field to just fly down and pick up the seed. Jesus explains things further in Mark 4:15, *"And these are the ones by the wayside where the Word is sown. When they hear, Satan comes immediately and takes away the Word that was sown in their hearts."*

When you have a hard heart, it's easy for Satan to just take the Word by force. You just forget what was taught or what you studied and don't remember what the Word said. So we see the birds in the parable are actually representative of Satan stealing the Word immediately when we have a hard, "packed down" heart that is not conducive for producing a crop.

People come to church to hear the Word and rarely take time to make sure there's no hardness in their hearts. In 1 Corinthians 11:31, Paul tells us, *"For if we would judge ourselves, we would not be judged."* Maybe a husband and wife are driving to church. They get into an argument about nothing and fuss all the way to the front door. They glare at one another, scowl, and promise that they'll finish the argument after church. Then the Pastor preaches about love, forgiveness, hardness of heart, and how Satan is trying to get an advantage in our lives in order to keep us fruitless and have our prayers hindered. (See 1 Peter 3:7.) But they don't hear a thing. They're still steaming over nothing. After church, they pick up right where they left off. Neither of them knows how they got there, but suddenly one issue has morphed into five other issues that were never settled. There is a cure for a hard heart. Its work to plow, till and work the ground, but the harvest demands the soil be in order or there will be no harvest.

Chapter 6
Satan and the Soil

Remember in Chapter 1 when we talked about the root of bitterness? Maybe your root is a divorce five years ago, but your heart has never really healed. So you carry around all the hurts from someone who has long gone, someone who has already moved on. Maybe it's time you move on too! If years ago, you were married to Tim and he hurt you, you have to be careful or that root will stay right in your heart. Then maybe a few years later, you meet Jim. Jim is a great guy. He encourages, loves and values you. But because you never really got that hurt out of your heart from Tim, you treat Jim as if he were Tim.

It's easy for Satan to steal the Word when people's hearts are hard. The Bible says he does it immediately. So that must mean Satan goes to church! He must ride in our cars and go to Bible studies with us. Anywhere we hear the Word; he must be there to challenge the Word with contrary thoughts and suggestions. Jesus states it clearly in John 10:10, *"The thief does not come except to steal, and to kill, and to destroy. I have come that they may have life, and that they may have it more abundantly."*

We've learned two things about the character of Satan: 1) He comes immediately to steal the Word from our hearts. 2) He's a thief that only comes to steal, kill and destroy. Let's learn another thing about our enemy: 3) He hates people whether they are Christians or not. That might seem like a bold statement, but think about it. He hates mankind because we've been created in the image and likeness of God and been given the authority and dominion to govern and control our lives. He wanted that kind of power and influence, but God placed it upon man, as the following Scriptures show:

Then God said, "Let Us make man in Our image,

according to Our likeness; let them have dominion over the fish of the sea, over the birds of the air, and over the cattle, over all the earth and over every creeping thing that creeps on the earth.' So God created man in His own image; in the image of God He created them; male and female He created them. Then God blessed them, and God said to them, 'Be fruitful and multiply; fill the earth and subdue it; have dominion over the fish of the sea, over the birds of the air, and over every living thing that moves on the earth." (Genesis 1:26-28)

So the Lord God said to the serpent: "Because you have done this, you are cursed more than all the cattle, and more than every beast of the field; on your belly you shall go, and you shall eat dust all the days of your life. And I will put enmity between you and the woman, and between your seed and her Seed; He shall bruise your head, and you shall bruise His heel." (Genesis 3:14-15)

🔑 We have to realize there's an enemy in the garden God created.

We must learn to guard and protect what God has given us. God never covers up man's sins and mistakes in the Bible in order to show us that we'll all blow it, and to prove that when we do, God's there to still help us. He knows we're just flesh.

🔑 We must stay vigilant about the enemy, about his tactics and plans to steal God's Word from our hearts.

God shows us that Satan comes with arguments, reasoning and imaginations as part of his scams to influence us against God's Word, *"...lest Satan should take advantage of us; for we are not ignorant of his devices."* (2 Corinthians 2:11)

"For though we walk in the flesh, we do not war according to the flesh. For the weapons of our warfare are not carnal, but mighty in God for pulling down strongholds, casting down arguments and every high thing that exalts itself against the knowledge of God, bringing every thought into captivity to the obedience of Christ." (2 Corinthians 10:3-5)

In the Amplified Bible, 2 Corinthians 10:5 reads,

"[Inasmuch as we] refute arguments and theories and reasonings and every proud and lofty thing that sets itself up against the [true] knowledge of God; and we lead every thought and purpose away captive into the obedience of Christ (the Messiah, the Anointed One)."

I love what it says in the Amplified Bible: we should refute every argument, theory and reasoning that sets itself up against the knowledge of God. Make up your mind, that God's Word is your final authority! The enemy's plan is to keep people from hearing the Word. If he can't keep you from hearing the Word, then he'll try and deceive you into keeping junk in the same heart in which the Word has been planted. If he can't fill your heart with junk he will try and make you "a flake" or strange so you can't relate with others. But understand this for certain, Satan has a plan to separate you from the life in the Word.

All farmers not only plow their fields, but as they plow, rocks and other debris are brought to the surface from where they were buried underground. A plow can dig down over a foot deep to turn the soil over. That's what the Word of God, prayer and study does to our hearts. That's what staying in the Word and being pliable before the Lord does. We're able to recognize attitudes or convictions or deceptions that may be wrong. Yes, you may be sincere about your belief and attitudes, but you also may be sincerely wrong. The Word exposes hard places in our hearts. Satan's plan is to keep you ineffective, to keep you filled with everything but a pure heart.

Maybe you're already a Christian. You know you've trusted God through Christ for eternal life, but maybe you're still mean as a snake. Maybe it's your ethics in business or lusts in your heart that need confronting. Farmers must get the rocks out of the field if they intend to get the harvest they want. The farmer prepares the soil (heart) with the harvest in mind.

When we go to church or study God's Word on our own, it's the equivalent of the farmer plowing, disking and pulling the rocks from the field. As we continue this teaching, we'll learn less is more when it comes to the heart; less hardness, fewer rocks and debris, fewer thorns.

🔑 All of this means fewer competing elements to threaten the life of the seed that's going into the soil.

This might seem like overkill, but if you're going to produce spiritual fruit like the farmer wants to produce crops in the field, then soil and heart preparation is a necessity.

🔑 Satan is coming to steal the Word out of your heart. (Mark 4:15)

Now I don't want anyone to be so demon and devil conscious that they lose their confidence in God, but the Bible says in 1 Peter 5:8, *"Be sober, be vigilant; because your adversary the devil walks about like a roaring lion, seeking whom he may devour."* Make up your mind that you are not one he can manipulate or devour.

Satan's job is to sow all kinds of hardness into your hearts. Hardness can take the form of jealousy, drama, unforgiveness, lust and even hatred. Once you become a Christian, Satan will use people to do some really hateful things to you. People can say really hurtful things and if we're not careful, even hatred or revenge can get into our hearts. He's looking for any opportunity to keep you from becoming good ground that produces fruit. Richard Nixon said, "those who hate you don't win unless you hate them [back]."

In military terms, they say that the best defense is a good offense. If you just renew your thinking and change some thought processes, you'll have a good offense against the devil. He's crafty, but you can learn to outthink him. *"lest Satan should take advantage of us; for we are not ignorant of his devices."* (2 Corinthians 2:11) We know he's going to use reasoning, thoughts, and arguments contrary to what God's Word says. He'll shoot thoughts at you at 100 miles per hour to get you thinking about anything other than God's plan for your situation.

So how exactly do we combat these thoughts? The following Scriptures tell us how:

"I beseech you therefore, brethren, by the mercies of God, that you present your bodies a living sacrifice, holy, acceptable to God, which is your reasonable service. And do not be conformed to this world, but be transformed by the renewing of your mind, that you may prove what is that good and acceptable and perfect will of God." (Romans 12:1-2)

"Therefore, take up the whole armor of God, that you may be able to withstand in the evil day, and having done all, to stand. Stand therefore." (Ephesians 6:13)

We'll have opportunities to get weak and shaken during the standing process. Be committed to stand in the face of the storms and reasonings that come against you. You and God make the majority, and you will reap if you don't faint!

"But those who wait on the Lord shall renew their strength; They shall mount up with wings like eagles; They shall run and not be weary; They shall walk and not faint." (Isaiah 40:31)

We are warned in Hebrews not to cast away our confidence, which has great reward. Don't cast away your confidence!

One translation says not to wad up your confidence and throw it away. Sometimes I have to see God move and bring His will to pass in a seemingly no win situation. I'm sure you've experienced God's delivering ability at least one time in your walk. When you get the hardness out of your heart, you're bound to win your battles. Just give the seed a chance to grow. The disciples saw mighty miracles, but still had some hardness in their hearts. They failed under pressure. They forgot the miracle of the loaves and fishes. (See Mark 6:37-44.)

Matthew 13:19 reads, *"When anyone hears the word of the kingdom and does not understand it, then the wicked one comes and snatches away what was sown in his heart. This is he on whom received seed by the wayside."* Satan can only steal or snatch away the Word if we don't understand or believe it. Therefore, it is to our advantage if we spend a quantity and quality time in hearing and understanding the truth of God's Word.

I grew up in a mainstream denomination that never encouraged me to read my Bible. I was never told about study, prayer or renewing my mind. So I couldn't stay in that spiritual environment if I wanted to grow and develop. You might ask, Pastor Dan, are you telling me to leave my church? No, I'm saying that I had to because my priority was growth and victory, overcoming and helping others to do the same. My future and my development is hinged on right information and being able to understand it. Satan can only steal the Word if you don't understand it.

In Bible school, the president and founder of the college would teach us each week. He said many times that even an old cow had enough sense to eat the hay and spit out the sticks. Then he would say wouldn't it be better to go where there are no sticks? Your spiritual future is too important to waste on teaching that isn't 100% Biblical. I don't listen to preachers that are accurate some of the time. I study people and subjects that are consistently scriptural.

To believe something just because it's traditional is crazy. There are whole denominations that don't know why they believe some things. I have a relative that was raised in a denominational church where they would place the names of sick people on a chalk board. Everyone would be asked to pray for Brother So and So to be healed if it were the Lord's will for him to be healed. He went through this ritual, and his father died. I never forgot that story because I wanted to know the significance of the chalk board. The prayer was total unbelief. Find out what God's will is concerning any subject and then pray in faith. I never did find the significance of the chalkboard. Putting faith in a chalk board or anything else other than God's promises is deception.

God covers His will all through the Bible. I heard someone say that God is mysterious. No, He's not. You can't write sixty-six books telling your followers what you will and will not do, publish those books so that they become the #1 best seller of all time and still be mysterious. He does exactly what He said He'd do. Understanding God's will is as simple as reading and believing the Bible. Cold dead religion is the art of making the simple things of God difficult.

Remember Matthew 13:19 in the Amplified Bible:

"While anyone is hearing the Word of the kingdom and does not grasp and comprehend it, the evil one comes and snatches away what was sown in his heart. This is what was sown along the roadside."

We should spend whatever time is necessary to get a good working understanding of God's Word. John 8:31-32 says,

"Then Jesus said to those Jews who believed in Him, 'If you abide in My word, you are My disciples indeed. And you shall know the truth, and the truth shall make you free." It's only the truth that makes us free.

If we don't understand the Word, Satan comes to steal it.

I was at a church service in Tulsa when I was a new Christian. The service was great; the teaching was informational and inspirational. A few days later, I dropped by the church and saw one of the pastors. I commented about the previous Sunday's message and how good it was. He asked me what the minister spoke on. I said, "Well, it was good..." And then I drew a blank. You see, I had forgotten. Even though the message was good and inspiring, Satan stole it from me because of a lack of focus and single-mindedness. I didn't understand it so I lost it. The minister who was teaching had revelation on the subject. But I didn't take the time and effort for it to become my revelation and Satan just stole the Word like a bird taking a seed off the hard road.

The lock that will keep you out of God's best is lack of understanding.

🔑 Focus fosters understanding.

If you want understanding and a heart that is good ground, travel light. What do you mean Danny? I mean understanding will flow when you're not carrying unforgiveness, hatred, fear and hopelessness in your heart. Let all those heavy burdens go. They will just choke all the life out of you. One key to understanding the Word is in Mark 4:10: *"But when He was alone, those around Him with the twelve asked Him about the parable."* They asked for explanations when they were alone with Him. When was the last time you asked God privately how the Kingdom works? We all like the public church service. We like to see and be seen. But just like a plant in the field, most of our growing happens below the surface in privacy. Yes, we want to look good. Who doesn't? But we should be more concerned with what happens when no one sees, when it's just you and a private audience with the Master.

Spending time with God through study and prayer makes you more sensitive to Him and His desire for your life. That makes sense. If you want to get to know someone better, you have to invest time. If you're dating someone and it's looking as if it's going to be a serious long term relationship, spend long hours communicating in many different environments: formal dinners, social outings, family get-togethers. You really get to know each other the more you spend time together. The same is true with God. Take private time when it's just you and Him, just like the disciples did in Mark 4:10, *"But when He was alone, those around Him with the twelve asked Him about the parable."* Read His Word, it's like looking into a mirror. Then you can begin to deal with the hardness and stony ground in your heart. If you want to be the farmer who produces a crop, it will take time and effort.

I've known a few national and world champion body builders. They were huge! They got that way because they had a passion for the sport, good genetics and were willing to take the time and effort to be great. They had to order their whole lives around their passion. Diet, exercise, rest, and weight training, their whole lives were scheduled around meeting their goals. You don't think they got twenty plus inch biceps by seeing a dime on the ground and merely picking it up, do you? No, it took hours and hours of concentrated, isolated effort over years to achieve those "guns"! If your heart is to be free from hardness and stones and to become fertile ground that ultimately bears Kingdom fruit, you'll have to be dedicated. Cut out a lot of nonsense; concentrate and isolate your heart to ensure that you're sensitive to God.

🔑 It takes effort to stay sensitive to the Lord.

Satan's plan for you is to stay busy, unorganized and undisciplined with your bible study and church attendance. Your personal growth must be a priority. The enemy has a plan to trip you up. God has a plan to grow you up.

In Mark 4:14-15, Jesus told his disciples,

"The sower sows the Word. And these are the

ones by the wayside where the Word is sown. When
they hear, Satan comes immediately and takes away
the Word that was sown in their hearts."

We've learned that the wayside is a hard packed road
and that Satan is represented as the "birds" that come and
take the Word. The Greek word used for take means to take
by force, meaning the Word is taken by force. Satan doesn't
play fair. When you're unsaved or saved but not particularly
interested in the things of God, your hard heart makes it
possible for Satan to take the seed by force. He's like a bully
that picks on the young, the weak and the sick. It's easy for
the bully to steal from those who are hard hearted.

Hard heartedness is explained best in Mark 4:13, *"And*
He said to them, 'Do you not understand this parable? How
then will you understand all the parables?'" When we don't
understand the Word or God's Kingdom process, Satan comes
and takes advantage of our ignorance. The very thing that
can help us with our hard hearts is the Word, and he steals
it, taking it by force.

When I was about ten or eleven, there was a bully in our
neighborhood. He used to take my lunch money and not let
me walk down the road to my house. One day I stood up to
him and punched him in the face. He never took my lunch
money again. Not because I was a good fighter or brave,
I wasn't either of those things. He didn't take my lunch money
anymore because I stood up to him. Once you get that hard
heart out of the way, and you become soft and pliable before
God, Satan can't come by force anymore to push you around.
Understanding is the key. When you know your rights as a
citizen of the U.S., you won't let anyone deny your freedom
of speech or your right to worship and other civil liberties.
If you don't know your rights, people will take advantage of
you. In the same way, it's only when our hearts are as hard
as the road that Satan can bully us. We'll explore the remedy
to a hard heart. It all has to do with what we think about.

Chapter 7
Stony Ground

"Some fell on stony ground, where it did not have much earth; and immediately it sprang up because it had no depth of earth. But when the sun was up it was scorched, and because it had not root it withered away."
Mark 4:5-6

Becoming and remaining good ground is neither chance nor a coincidence, *but a choice*. I'm convinced that if we put as much time into working the ground of our hearts as a farmer does his fields, we will be the people we've always dreamt about; people whose prayers are being answered more frequently. We can become people with the favor of God upon our lives evident for all to see. We will be happier and have more optimistic attitudes with a great uplook as well as outlook. It is possible; as possible as a diligent farmer taking care and maintaining the soil of his farm. It's not too good to be true. It's not a pipe dream or wishing upon a star, you are responsible for the condition of your heart.

ꙮ Stony ground is almost as difficult to grow crops in as the road or wayside.

The Greek Word for stony ground literally means 'ground full of stones'. Picture that in your mind's eye. Picture a field full of rocks. Wouldn't it be difficult for a farmer to expect or grow a crop with the field full of rocks? Sure. But Christians do it all the time when it comes to their hearts.

That's exactly what the Bible teaches. The seed without much soil immediately sprang up because there was no depth. This is so interesting if you understand anything about agriculture. You can take two identical seeds and put them in identical conditions – the same water, fertilizer, sunlight,

77

same quality of soil, etc. The only measurable difference would be the depth of the soil in which you planted them. One seed was planted in a pot with a foot of soil, and another in a pot with an inch of soil. The interesting fact is that the seed planted in an inch of soil will spring up and grow much sooner than the one that has twelve inches of soil in the pot. The shallow seed will spring up above ground after several days, while the one with twelve inches of soil may not seem to be making any progress for a much longer period of time.

Why? Because it is growing down before it ever grows up. Note to self, we don't want to be the one that springs up right away but can't sustain the growth. The root system has twelve inches of soil to grow in as a foundation. The seed in one inch of soil has but one inch of depth, so it springs up quickly. It has very little root system, and any weight, breeze or insect will topple the plant because it has no root system developed underground. Sure the seed with one inch of soil broke the surface of the ground first, but for the farmer, growing a healthy corn plant is more important. It's not a race to see what looks the best from the outside. That's the problem with many believers. They don't care about the roots or the health of their heart. They just want to look good. In reality, the farmer makes sure the field is free of rocks because he's interested in his corn having a developed root system. Good roots guarantee good fruit.

Mark 4:5-6 is further explained in verses 16-18:

"These likewise are the ones sown on stony ground who, when they hear the Word, immediately receive it with gladness; and they have no root in themselves, and so endure only for a time. Afterward, when tribulation or persecution arises for the Word's sake, immediately they stumble."

These verses describe the believers who hear the Word with their hearts full of stones. They receive it with gladness. In other words, they are emotional about it. That's great, but this is not an emotional gospel. A farmer doesn't have to get emotional about the seed, the ground or the harvest. Emotions are not really part of the process unless you're just looking for an escape. Emotions come and go, but the Word of God works whether we feel good or bad. My emotions are a product of what I think about, and I can change moods by what I focus on. Some people never get over hurts from their past. As a matter of fact, prisons are full of people who couldn't get over hurts or couldn't control their emotions. It is amazing to watch so many people wind up in trouble or die because of lack of control over their emotions. The other day I saw a show that featured a teenager who shot and killed his friend. The boy who was being interviewed said, "I didn't kill him, he's my friend." But, the police had enough corroborating evidence to charge him with the murder. The outcome was that one boy offended the other and someone couldn't control his emotions.

I have a file at my office labeled "Hate Mail". They are letters and E-mails from congregants, letters from radio listeners and TV viewers. Some of these letters are so vicious you'd never think a true believer could say those things to another true believer. Years ago if I was having a melancholy day, I'd take out my hate mail and have a good pity party, which of course made my day even worse. "I'm so bad. I can't do anything right. All these people are right. I think I'll just go eat a rotten egg." After a few times of repeating that process, my lightening fast mind figured out that those letters and emails were hurting me, not helping me. I had to stop the nonsense. I learned my emotions were things that had to be controlled and managed.

The people in Mark 4:16-18 were emotional about the Word. They were glad to hear it. But it takes a commitment to the Word of God to overcome, regardless of whether you feel good or bad.

🔑 You and God make the majority.

In verse 17, the emotional people who heard the Word planted it in a heart full of stones and therefore could not produce a root system strong enough to withstand the pressures of life. Mark 4:15 taught us that when the Word is heard, Satan comes to steal it. He does so through the issues of life putting pressure on your root system once you've heard the Word; or through tribulation and persecution for the Word's sake. Satan uses the pressures of life to separate you from the lifeline of the promises of God.

The quality of the plant can be found in its ability to produce under pressure. Pressure reveals the root system. Here in Florida we deal with the threat of hurricanes just about every year. Hurricane Charlie was awful. Many of our congregants had damage to their homes and businesses. My secretary's house was devastated. You know what was amazing? Many times you'd see large trees blown right over while the palm trees survived. Palm trees' root systems are designed to go through strong storms. We had a huge tree blown over on the church property because it had a shallow root system. Not the palm trees. They grow so deep they can withstand 140 mph winds.

A tree can't live off of another tree's root system; they must make their own. The same is true of you and me. I can't live off of someone else's commitment to God. I can't depend on someone else developing strong roots. I can only be strong and produce fruit if I take the time to focus on the Word for myself.

In my own life, I have made sure to have a strong root system. I study the Word daily. I pray and put time into my relationship with God. This focused effort ensures that when some little problem, trouble or temptation comes along, it can't topple my relationship with God. I've put in a huge amount of time to guarantee stability—even in a storm.

I won't backslide because I have a daily walk with God. Now if I were to stop studying, stop praying and meditating on God's Word, I could be messed up in just a few months' time. If I neglect God and substitute carnal things for Him, I could reap a negative harvest. So I'll just keep the Word close and overcome.

"As you have therefore received Christ Jesus the Lord, so walk in Him, rooted and built up in Him and established in the faith, as you have been taught, abounding in it with thanksgiving." (Colossians 2:6-7)

"Be diligent to present yourself approved to God, a worker who does not need to be ashamed, rightly dividing the word of truth." (2 Timothy 2:15)

The enemy brings afflictions and persecutions because he wants to stop any potential fruit. He wants to affect the process of growth and development before it really gets rooted. He is a manipulator and wants to keep as many Christians with stony hearts as he can. Let's talk about the why of persecution and afflictions. They come to you, to make you stumble. In the Amplified Bible Mark 4:17 reads:

"And they have no real root in themselves, and so they endure for a little while; then when trouble or persecution arises on the account of the Word, they immediately are offended (become displeased, indignant, resentful) and they stumble and fall away."

The plan of the enemy is to get you offended so you'll stop hearing the Word.

There are four 'D's that will keep you from continuing in the truth:

1. Discouragement. Dis-courage. One of our great assets as children of God is the courage we take from knowing that our God lives. Read Joshua 1:2-9 if you want some encouragement. If we remember God is alive and with us, we won't let discouragement get its teeth into us.

2. Distractions.

🔑 Distractions keep you from seeing when you get your eyes off the vision.

Focus is a powerful force. Peter walked on the water while focused on Jesus, but when he was distracted by the wind and the waves, he began to sink, *"But when he saw that the wind was boisterous, he was afraid; and beginning to sink he cried out, saying, 'Lord, save me!'"* (Matthew 14:30) Never get distracted by factors that don't matter. Peter was already walking on the water. What difference did it make if there was thunder and lightening?

3. Delays.

🔑 Delay doesn't mean denial.

Remember Genesis 8:22, *"While the earth remains, seedtime and harvest, cold and heat, winter and summer, and day and night shall not cease."* When delays happen they can get you discouraged and distracted enough that you lose focus. There's always going to be a time period in the process. You must understand the process so the enemy can't use delays against you.

4. Deception.

The enemy is a liar and the father of lies. John 8:44 says, *"When he speaks a lie, he speaks it from his own resources, for he is a liar and the father of it."* He can manipulate things in this natural realm, so we need to cling tightly to what God has said, *"Lest Satan should take advantage of us; for we are not ignorant of his devices."* (2 Corinthians 2:11) In the last days, Satan will even try to deceive the elite.

🔑 We must focus on God's Word so we won't become a casualty of deception.

We can easily see that persecution and affliction have one goal, and that is to keep us from producing fruit and to keep us offended. Offended people never further the Kingdom's mission. Let's choose to grow. If your heart isn't good ground, work on it. If you have shallow soil full of rocks, hardness, thorns, thistles and drama; work on it. God's on your side. Stony ground is a result of an uninvolved farmer who has lost focus and forgot about the harvest. If you and I have a vision of a fruitful harvest, we must ensure our heart isn't full of stones. Only you have control of your heart and its condition.

This process of good ground will work for you. Don't let discouragement, distractions, delays or deceptions affect the quality of your heart. It is too important to leave it unattended or under maintained. Don't let offences in your heart. I've never met a happy offended person. Have you?

Chapter 8
Thorny Ground

"And some seed fell among thorns; and the thorns grew up and choked it, and it yielded no crop" (Mark 4:7).

It's amazing how weeds and thorns just seem to grow by themselves without any effort from the farmer. In fact the farmer actually has to put a great deal of time and energy into keeping the weeds out of his field, because they'll spring up all over the place on their own. As keeper of your heart, you must be vigilant to protect your own soil.

🔑 No farmer ever expects their field to be free of weeds on its own.

Nor does a farmer expect his field to be weed free or rock free just because he is in the farming business. From past experience he has learned that he must till the ground.

So many Christians hold God responsible for what they're going through. They say, "God, if you really loved me, my life would be easier." Or, "If I was in your perfect will, things would be smoother." If that was the case, then Peter, Paul and Jesus himself never made it into the perfect will of God. Taking responsibility for one's actions is one of the first signs or indicators of maturity. Wherever Jesus went there was either revival or a riot. Psalm 34:19 says, *"Many are the afflictions of the righteous, but the LORD delivers him out of them all."*

🔑 You are responsible for the condition of your heart.

Why is this so important? Because verse 7 clearly states that thorns choke the corps. The result is no harvest. Some of you just got mad at me because I shifted the responsibility of your heart to you. If your heart is filled with strife, lust, drama and unbelief, it's your fault! Is that plain enough? What would you think of a farmer leaning on his tractor, crying to his farmer friends about the condition of his fields? "I don't know why God has allowed my fields to be full of rocks, weeds and thorns. I guess God's just punishing me." Don't think for a minute that the farmer's friends would pat him on the back and say, "Poor soul, you're just being persecuted. This must be some huge demonic attack against your field." No, they'd tell him that you can't grow a crop through sympathy or blame. You'll never get the harvest if you don't do something about the hard ground, the rocks and the thorns. They would also tell that farmer, "You know better than to blame others for the condition of your field. Now get on your tractor and get busy doing what you know only you can do!" The condition of your field is entirely the result of your preparation.

🔑 We live in a culture that refuses to take responsibility.

We blame everything and everyone else rather than looking in the mirror. Adam and Eve were the first to start the blame game. Adam said the woman you gave me told me to eat the fruit and Eve said the serpent deceived me (Genesis 3:11-13). They started the excuse mill and somehow year after year it's been passed down to the next generation. Isn't it funny how excuses and blame have been perfected in some families? Excuses are the vocabulary of the unsuccessful and jealous. Don't be that person.

I deal with people all day, and I see that some people take responsibility for their actions and some don't. Years ago I was called in the middle of the night because there had been a terrible auto accident involving a youth whose family were casual attenders of our church. When I say casual, I mean they attended a few times a year. As soon as I arrived at the emergency room, I saw that family members of both the parties who had been involved were present. The casual attendees of our church learned that their child was fine. Once the fear of serious injury was lifted, they immediately began to circle the wagons and make excuses for their son's driving. Meanwhile, the other family was mourning the death of their child. Police were involved now and the investigation had started.

I stepped back and asked the police officer what had happened. It seemed that the son of the occasional attendees was at fault. He had been driving recklessly and caused the accident. Once I knew the full story, I got the family together, and I told them to stop the excuses. "Your son was at fault, and there is another family grieving a few feet away because of your son's actions. I'm going over there to help that family cope with the loss." The casual attending family later tried to get me to be a character witness in court for their son. I declined and encouraged them to take responsibility for their son's actions. What a terrible example the parents set for their teenager. For fear of a lawsuit, they decided to blame and not take responsibility. Their hearts had some stones.

When Joselyn and I were just dating, I was following her in my car as we were going to a restaurant for a meal. I saw a young child walking a dog ahead of her. The dog began to pull against the leash, got out of its collar and darted across the street. The child instinctively ran after the dog and right in front of Joselyn's car. She swerved to miss the child and ended up totaling her car. She had to go in an ambulance for observation with some minor injuries. As the ambulance was preparing to leave, I quickly walked a few houses away to where the young girl ran back after she retrieved the dog. I confronted the parents and thought they would be appreciative of Joselyn's sacrificing her car and physical well being. The parents, to my surprise, said it wasn't their child or dog involved, even though both were right there in the living room when they answered the door. What an example for the child. I hope their example didn't cost them too much over the years. (Children learn at home.)

Some people will blame everyone else for their actions. The condition of a farmer's field is totally within his power and under his control. If he doesn't want the rocks in the field, he will pick them up. If he doesn't like the weeds, he pulls them up. He doesn't complain about the condition of the field when it is in his power to do something about it!

My wife, Joselyn, and I were just in New Jersey, speaking at our home church. We had dinner at a restaurant and met a lady there. She had emigrated from Nigeria some twenty years before. She told us how she was putting her daughter through medical school, and that her daughter was almost finished. I sat there and thought, 'Here's a single mom from Africa. She's worked here legally for twenty years and raised a child who is going through medical school. She never mentioned the hardships she'd been through.' She didn't highlight the two jobs and all the sacrifices she'd made. I was impressed. If there was someone who could have found an excuse not to achieve, it would have been this woman. Here's a lesson: If you find excuses, *don't pick them up*. If your heart isn't in the condition conducive for growing crops, correct it!

Haven't we all met people that had a horrible childhood and could never get over it? They seem to talk about it every single time you have a conversation with them. After a while, you could tell their story as well as them because you've heard it so many times. Those bad experiences have evidently grown deep into their hearts and taken root, and now every life experience runs through those roots. Remember Proverbs 4:23, *"Keep your heart with all diligence, for out of it spring the issues of life."* It's up to you to keep all the issues of life from contaminating your heart. Just like the weeds grow without any help, the issues of life grow in hard hearts, stony and thorny ground. There was an old TV commercial around thirty years ago that featured Smoky Bear saying, "Only YOU can prevent forest fires." That's also true about your life. Only you can control what is in your heart. You can break strongholds in your mind and life can start anew. Bring your thoughts in line with God's Word. (See 2 Corinthians 10:4-5.)

If you are not diligent, thorns grow and choke the life and potential out of the good seed. Let's read Mark 4:18-19, which explains verse 7 further:

"Now these are the ones sown among thorns; they are the ones who hear the Word, and the cares of this world, the deceitfulness of riches, and the desires for other things entering in choke the word, and it becomes unfruitful."

🔑 Satan can't stop you from hearing the Word.

The key is that life is in the seed, the Word. The enemy can't stop you from hearing the Word of God (See Mark 4:23.). This is definitely the key to victory in all our lives. Keep on hearing the Word—no matter if times are good or bad, happy or sad; keep hearing the Word. If the seas in your life are rough or calm, keep hearing. There's life in the Word so if you have ears to hear, keep hearing. Once you've heard it, Satan will try yet again to get you focused on all the wrong stuff, on cares, on the deceitfulness of riches and on lusts of all kinds. Let's examine these three stumbling blocks, so we won't get tripped up. After all, *it's our desire to bear fruit.* John 15:16 says,

"You did not choose Me, but I chose you and appointed you that you should go and bear fruit, and that your fruit should remain, that whatever you ask the Father in My name, He may give you."

1. Cares:

The Greek word means 'to divide the mind' and includes distractions, worries, burdens, and anxieties. The word care means to be anxious beforehand about your daily life. That's what our enemy tries to sell us on.

🔑 He wants you to worry about tomorrow when you're not even there yet.

It's useless to waste time with fears about tomorrow, to blow them up in our minds and dwell on them. We make mountains out of molehills. Jesus teaches about this very subject and helps us to see the futility of worry in Matthew 6:25-32:

> *"Therefore I say to you, do not worry about your life, what you will eat or what you will drink; nor about your body, what you will put on. Is not life more than food and the body more than clothing? Look at the birds of the air, for they neither sow nor reap nor gather into barns; yet your heavenly Father feeds them. Are you not of more value than they? Which of you by worrying can add one cubit to his stature? So why do you worry about clothing? Consider the lilies of the field, how they grow: they neither toil nor spin; and yet I say to you that even Solomon in all his glory was not arrayed like one of these. Now if God so clothes the grass of the field, which today is, and tomorrow is thrown into the oven, will He not much more clothe you, O you of little faith? Therefore, do not worry, saying, 'What shall we eat?' or 'What shall we drink?' or 'What shall we wear?' For after all these things the Gentiles seek. For your heavenly Father knows that you need all these things."*

God also gives the remedy for these anxious thoughts that choke out the Word in Matthew 6:33-34,

> *"But seek first the kingdom of God and His righteousness, and all these things shall be added to you. Therefore do not worry about tomorrow, for tomorrow will worry about its own things. Sufficient for the day is its own trouble."*

God knows about the mess you can get yourself into by concentrating on negative thoughts. When you worry about your bills, children, job, future and health, it robs you of the strength to live in the moment. Worrying releases chemicals in your body that will push you into an emotional funk that can lead to depression.

That's why it's imperative that we do what Philippians 4:8 says,

"Finally, brethren, whatever things are true, whatever things are noble, whatever things are just, whatever things are pure, whatever things are lovely, whatever things are of good report, if there is any virtue and if there is anything praiseworthy— meditate on these things."

Think on the right things. It's a physiological fact that smiling has an effect on your outlook. It's not good for you to look back on all the bad things that have happened in your life and dwell on them.

You can't live in the past and see your future.

Your car has a big windshield to look through as you're driving forward. What is behind you is not quite as important. There's a little rear view mirror in every car so that periodically you can glance behind. What's out in front of you is so much more important than some of the junk you have already passed. Yes, learn from the past, but look forward.

Cares and worries will contaminate your future.

2. The Deceitfulness of Riches

If we're not careful, we'll replace our trust and confidence in God with the deception that money can fix anything. Instead of "In God We Trust," we replace it with "In Money We Trust." That's a fantasy to think we can trust or find security in money. The Bible tells us that no one can serve both God and money. Money can't love you back. It can't die for you; it never forgave you. In reality, money is just a tool. Money takes on your character. Many years ago, a minister received a large donation from a gentleman here in Florida who owned a dog track. Out of the goodness of his heart, the dog track owner wanted to bless the ministry during a time of need. It was wild to see how the church at large dealt with that donation. Many people and churches stopped supporting the ministry because they said it was dirty money, gambling money. But money is amoral; it was neither good nor bad. It simply takes on the character of the recipient. The minister used the money to spread the gospel, help the poor, train college students, and support other good projects.

Money is a tool. It is not a god. It is to be used to reach the world with the gospel. Riches can lie to you. If you're not careful, they will deceive you into thinking that if you get enough money, you won't have to trust in God. The carnal nature can't be trusted. The carnal nature wants us to rely on the deceitfulness of riches and on ourselves and others, not on God or Kingdom principles. Jesus said in Luke 12:15-21,

"And He said to them, "Take heed and beware of covetousness, for one's life does not consist in the abundance of the things he possesses." Then He spoke a parable to them, saying,

"The ground of a certain rich man yielded plentifully. And he thought within himself, saying, 'What shall I do, since I have no room to store my crops?' So he said, 'I will do this: I will pull down my barns and build greater, and there I will store all my crops and my goods. And I will say to my soul, 'Soul, you have many goods laid up for many years; take your ease; eat, drink and be merry.' But God said to him, 'Fool! This night your soul will be required of you; then whose will those things be which you have provided?' So is he who lays up treasure for himself,

and is not rich toward God."

When you get your prosperity, it's not time to take it easy and forget your God. Riches will lie to you if you allow them to. We've all seen the old cartoon of the monkey. There are three scenes. One has the monkey dressed up in a tuxedo with the caption under the picture, "I've been rich." The next scene has the monkey sitting on a curb with old tattered clothes on and the caption reads, "And I've been poor." The next comic scene caption states, "rich is better."

Many of us can say the same thing in differing degrees. Rich or having more than enough is better. I've been on both sides of the cartoon. If you're not careful, money will give you a false sense of security. During these trying economic times, there is a lot of pressure to trust in money or a job or whatever. (See Psalm 20:7.) We've seen lots of folk cut back on their giving when they hit crunch time. It's sad when people trust money more than God. Why would we cut back on our giving just because times seem tough? That is the time to double up.

Giving is a great way to keep that in check. When money lies to you and tells you that you can put your trust in it to secure your future, it's time to give so no trust is placed in anything but God and His promises.

Many years ago, our church was in a building program. Things got tight in Florida and people began to waver in their giving. Jos and I decided not to take a salary from the church to be an example to the folks how you can still trust God under pressure. Everything in me was saying to keep taking the salary but I knew my God and wanted to make a point. Months went by with no salary from the church but at the end of the year, we had given the church thousands of dollars in tithes and offering, not counting the other ministries we supported. Although we had received no salary during the first part of the year, we ended up giving over $10,000 of what we did make to the church.

It was a really good example of how God will supply our needs even under pressure. Sometimes you have to starve out those thoughts of trusting anything other than God and His provision.

3. The lust of other things

The lust of other things enters in and chokes the Word, and it becomes unfruitful. The word lust means a desire or longing for. Satan will try anything to keep you from the life promised in the Word of God. Cares, deceitfulness of riches and lust or desires and longings for other things enter into your heart. Your heart is the soil of your life. It's the field in which life is cultivated. If the Word entering in your heart bears fruit, then other things entering your heart bear fruit also. A longing, a desire for other things enter in, and you get a crop.

Maybe it's politics that has entered your heart. You won't miss an afternoon radio talk show. Once you get home the cable news dominates your eyes, ears and heart. Pretty soon you start believing that if one party is in power, it's all over! If a candidate is doing well in the poles, you are happy. That's all that's on your mind. *As if God doesn't raise one king up and put another down.* Maybe it's the country club or some sports or hobbies that enter your heart.

🔑 There's only room for one person at a time on the throne of your heart.

We have to be as diligent as a farmer in his field, when it comes to what we allow to enter our hearts. Our hearts are designed to be a place of fertile soil and will grow whatever we put in there. The question is, what are you allowing in?

Have you ever noticed that it's easy to read a novel or the newspaper or to watch the news on TV? But just sit down with your Bible, a concordance and a commentary and watch out! Your mind, which was focused on the plot of a novel or the box scores of the sports page, drifts as you read

Deuteronomy. While watching the news, you're engrossed by the day's events. But sit down to read the Bible, and the phone will ring six times with people who just have to speak with you right away. It's a no-brainer that the enemy hates for anyone to give themselves to the Word that gives life.

And Hebrews 2:1 warns us, *"Therefore we must give the more earnest heed to the things we have heard, lest we drift away."* The fight is over the life giving Word. The Word that once was sown in our hearts' fertile soil can produce an amazing life. What are some of the things that have either entered into your heart or are trying to? Do you have fear, stress, and the desire for other things trying to enter in? These are all distractions meant to get you to concentrate on anything other than the life giving Word.

"My son, give attention to my words; incline your ear to my sayings. Do not let them depart from your eyes; Keep them in the midst of your heart; For they are life to those who find them, and health to all their flesh. Keep your heart with all diligence, for out of it spring the issues of life." (Proverbs 4:20-23)

Keep your heart with all diligence. Keep it, guard it, and protect what goes into it. Whatever goes into your heart is going to grow. An extra marital affair doesn't start in the "no tell motel," but in the mind. It is thought about, and cultivated before the arrangements and rendezvous are ever made. It's rehearsed over and over again in the mind until finally the fruit appears, and then regret and condemnation pounce. But it all started by thoughts entering into the heart.

The desires and longing for anything can enter in and choke the Word and by this the Word becomes unfruitful. Someone in our church gave me a little story one day about a Native American Indian and his young son. He was telling his son about the power of thoughts and how they grow. He used an illustration of two wolves, one good and one bad. The son asked which wolf was the strongest. The father answered,

"The one who I feed is the strongest." Wow!

🔑 The thoughts you feed or allow to dwell in your heart get stronger.

Don't allow the lust of other things to enter into the fertile ground of your heart. You don't want that crop! See James 1:14-15.)

Chapter 9
Good Ground

"But other seed fell on good ground and yielded a crop that sprang up, increased and produced: some thirty-fold, some sixty, and some a hundred."
Mark 4:8

When I was a young man, I spent a little time on the farm. And it's was easy to see when someone put the requisite time in preparing their fields and when someone didn't. Any farmer I knew always took whatever time was necessary to make sure that the ground he was putting his expensive seed into was prepared to receive it. It wasn't by accident or coincidence that a field was properly maintained and prepared. Skipping any step of the process ensured the ground wouldn't be ready. Skipping steps would ultimately compromise the yield of the field. Leaving hard ground, huge dirt clods, stones, weeds or debris in the field would have a direct effect on the crop's yield. That's why the farmer spends hours plowing, disking, removing rock and debris, depositing fertilizer, and irrigating. Why? Because he is thinking about the harvest, and all the ground preparation is about the harvest.

Good ground has been prepared. Much attention and work has gone into the process. That is true in every area of life. Not to get ahead of myself here, but once the ground is prepared and the seed is sown, the farmer isn't surprised when he gets a great crop. When we prepare, it takes much of the guess work out of farming. There are many variables the farmer isn't in control of, but field preparation is one that he is completely in control of.

During the Dust Bowl days of the early 1930's, the farmers used incredible short sightedness, to think that they could use and abuse the soil without repercussions. Soil does not take care of itself; it must be maintained on purpose.

In the plains, the soil wasn't favorable for farming and any old technique couldn't be used there. It required specialized tilling and maintenance of the soil if the land and the crops were to be maximized. After the Dust Bowl decade, new techniques were devised so erosion of the soil wouldn't be repeated. The Dust Bowl decade was prolonged because the farmers kept repeating the same tilling practices that created the national disaster. It wasn't until the dust clouds reached Washington DC, that anyone really started to deal with the situation.

We're living in an environment that does not encourage spiritual fruitfulness. Therefore, new techniques must be discovered so as not to repeat the practices that have produced spiritual unfruitfulness.

There is a Dust Bowl of unfruitfulness and frustration covering the landscape of the Church today. Many Christians are mistreating the soil of their heart which will carry on the environment that leads to more frustration and lack of fruit. Repeating the same techniques will only continue the drought.

The Dust Bowl lasted many more years than it should have because no one was willing to change. Haven't you repeated some of the same practices and routines long enough without results? Let's declare an end to the drought, and stop using worthless or antiquated techniques. Like a cancer that must be removed, some of our old techniques of maintaining our soul must be changed. It's time to stop thinking that you are going to have peace, favor, blessing and an overall joyful viewpoint while subjecting your soul to drama, strife and negativity; because it is a fantasy.

Some Christians must perform surgery by cutting away at their souls. Watching TV shows filled with junk, sometimes 40 to 50 hours per week, can contaminate your soul. Likewise, listening to music that triggers all the wrong thoughts and emotions or looking at photographs, sometimes on the walls of our homes, can do the same. We must do something different if we're to get another result. It's never too late to dream a new dream and to start afresh in our heart.

If you've been using antiquated systems and methods to keep your heart's good ground, and you have been through cycles of depression and bad attitudes which seem to keep you in a constant state of apathy, let me encourage you to start anew. Find a mentor who is good ground and implement some new ideas and methods for a better life. After all, we only get one life and we all want to maximize it.

🔑 When we prepare, things just go well.

In Proverbs 6:6-8 we are told to,

"Go to the ant, you sluggard! Consider her ways and be wise, which, having no captain, overseer or ruler, provides her supplies in the summer, and gathers her food in the harvest." The ant prepares beforehand.

Whenever we both have room in our schedules, my brother Mike & I go fishing. Long before I arrive, he has everything prepared, and that ensures a safe, fulfilling day. The boat has two way radios, fuel, food, rods, bait and life preservers. Every contingency has been thought through. If it rains, there's gear. If the fish aren't biting, we have a back up location. Preparation is paramount.

In Mark 4:20, Jesus expounds on His teaching about good ground, *"But these are the ones sown on good ground, those who hear the word, accept it, and bear fruit: some thirty-fold, some sixty and some a hundred."* Those who are good ground hear the Word, understand and accept it. When the Word is planted into good ground, you can begin to expect a crop. Jesus tells us in John 14:6, *"I am the way, the truth, and the life. No one comes to the Father except through Me."* Note that Jesus said, *"I am THE way,"* not

"I am *A* way." When the Word of God becomes the final authority and top priority in your life, it is an indication that your heart is good ground.

Let's see good ground in action in Mark 5:22-36,

And behold, one of the rulers of the synagogue came, Jairus by name. And when he saw Him, he fell at His feet and begged Him earnestly, saying, "My little daughter lies at the point of death. Come and lay your hands on her, that she may be healed and she will live." So Jesus went with him, and a great multitude followed Him and thronged Him.

Now a certain woman had a flow of blood for twelve years, and had suffered many things from many physicians. She had spent all that she had and was no better, but rather grew worse. When she heard about Jesus, she came behind Him in the crowd and touched His garment. For she said, "If only I may touch His clothes, I shall be made well." Immediately, the fountain of her blood was dried up, and she felt in her body that she was healed of the affliction. And Jesus, immediately knowing in Himself that power had gone out of Him, turned around in the crowd and said, "Who touched My clothes?" But His disciples said to Him, "You see the multitude thronging You, and You say, "Who touched Me?"

And He looked around to see her who had done this thing. But the woman, fearing and trembling, knowing what had happened to her, came and fell down before Him and told Him the whole truth. And He said to her, "Daughter, your faith has made you well. Go in peace, and be healed of your affliction." While He was still speaking, some came from the ruler of the synagogue's house who said, "Your daughter is dead. Why trouble the Teacher any further?" As soon as Jesus heard the word that was spoken, He said to the ruler of the synagogue, "Do not be afraid; only believe."

Let's look at this situation closely. Jairus, a local leader in the synagogue, came to Jesus in response to a crisis. That was the first in a series of good moves. Have you ever turned first to someone or something other than God for help? I've been guilty of divided focus when the heat or pressure was on. Jairus' name literally means One whom Jehovah enlightens, and God lets us see that his first move was toward Jesus.

🗝 Jairus set the parameters for Jesus to move and heal his daughter.

He said, "Come and lay your hands on her that she may be healed and she may live." The next verse (verse 24) is great: *"So Jesus went with him..."* It's amazing how Jesus just left a crowd to help someone who had a spirit of faith. In 2 Corinthians 4:13, Paul writes, *"And since we have the same spirit of faith, according to what is written, 'I believed and therefore I spoke,' we also believe and therefore speak."*

Next Jairus and Jesus were interrupted by a woman who had heard and received God's Word (verses. 25-29). She acted on what she believed. She said, *"If only I touch His clothes, I shall be made well."* There's no ambiguity in that statement. The Scripture is clear. She had heard about Jesus and what He could do. She understood the Word and acted on it. Therefore she was healed. I love how the New Living Translation interprets Jesus' words in verse 30: *"Who deliberately touched Me?"* I'm sure that is what God is waiting for in many of our lives—a deliberate touch

🗝 A key to harvest—deliberate actions.

That's really what faith is; a deliberate act once we know what God's will is in any situation.

So much is going on here. In verses 35-36, the lady testifies of her healing, and Jairus gets some bad news. His daughter is dead. In response, Jesus tells Jairus *"Do not be afraid, only believe."* You mean we can believe and have unbelief working at the same time? Obviously we can, because Jesus said only to believe. You see, mixing unbelief with belief is like having the cares of the world mixed in with the Word of God. Other things or unbelief compete with the Word in our hearts, which can and will cause a negative effect or hinder our faith. Unbelief is one thing that causes a hard heart. Having unbelief, fear or strife in your life and trying to walk by faith at the same time is like trying to drive with your parking brakes on. (See James 3:16.)

Jesus was encouraging Jairus not to back down, only to believe. His child rose and walked because he turned first to Jesus and just believed, regardless of circumstances. In Mark Chapter 4:40-41 Jesus calms the sea and the winds while the disciples are in fear of their lives.

But he said to them, "Why are you so fearful? How is it that you have no faith?" And they feared exceedingly, and said to one another, "'Who can this be, that even the wind and the sea obey Him?"

There are scores of examples of people with good ground in the Bible; from Rahab, Daniel and David in the Old Testament to Peter, Paul, Mary and James in the New Testament.

Understand that the devil lies to all of us and tells us the same tired stories. "You're not good enough." "You've sinned." "You don't have enough faith." Anything the devil says to you is a lie, so let's just start with that. John 8:44 reads,

"He was a murderer from the beginning, and does not stand in the truth, because there is no truth in him. When he speaks a lie, he speaks from his own resources, for he is a liar and the father of it."

The devil lies because there is no truth in him, none whatsoever! You don't have to have a lot faith to move your biggest problems. Jesus himself said in Matthew 7:19 - 20

102

that you only need faith the size of a mustard seed to move trees and mountains. Your problems can be moved because the Lord said they can be.

The next thing to do is use all of that negative information against the accuser. When he says, "You're not good enough" or "You've sinned," Simply answer, "Yes! But my relationship with God has a lot more to do with who I am in Christ than who I am in the flesh." Paul reminds us in 2 Corinthians 5:17 that, *"Therefore, if anyone is in Christ, he is a new creation; old things have passed away; behold, all things have become new."*

I agree with my adversary. In many cases I'm not good enough. But thank God I don't have to be! In some situations, I may have sinned, but thank God I'm still the righteousness of God in Christ. I have the faith of God, and that is more than enough for any project here on Earth. Sin is not the issue, Jesus is the issue. Mark 11:22-24 tells us,

"So Jesus answered and said to them, "Have faith in God. For assuredly, I say to you, whoever says to this mountain, "Be removed and be cast into the sea,' and does not doubt in his heart, but believes that those things he says will be done, he will have whatever he says. Therefore I say to you, whatever things you ask when you pray, believe that you receive them, and you will have them."

It's not about who we are in the flesh, but who Jesus is and what He's done for us. Let's take a look at another person. She was a young girl, and she was good ground. She heard the Word of God, believed it, received it, and brought forth a good harvest for mankind. Let us note she was a young person. She had never been to Bible school, and many people would consider her to be immature, both as a person and as a believer. (Which, by the way, is good news for the rest of us?) She just believed and took the Lord at His Word in Luke 1:26-31 & 34,

Now in the sixth month the angel Gabriel was

sent by God to a city of Galilee named Nazareth, to a virgin betrothed to a man whose name was Joseph, of the house of David. The virgin's name was Mary. And having come in, the angel said to her, "Rejoice, highly favored one, the Lord is with you; blessed are you among women!"

But when she saw him, she was troubled at his saying, and considered what manner of greeting this was. Then the angel said to her, "Do not be afraid, Mary, for you have found favor with God. And behold, you will conceive in your womb and bring forth a Son, and shall call His name Jesus." Then Mary said to the angel, "How can this be, since I do not know a man?"

Young Mary proved she was good ground. In verse 34, she asked a legitimate question. She was saying, 'I know how things work between a man and a woman to have a baby, and I've never known a man.' She asked, 'How are you going to do it, Lord?' Here is the reply in verses 35-38:

And the angel answered and said to her, "The Holy Spirit will come upon you, and the power of the Highest will overshadow you; therefore, also, that the Holy One who is to be born will be called the Son of God. Now indeed, Elizabeth your relative has also conceived a son in her old age; and this is now the sixth month for her who was called barren. For with God nothing will be impossible." Then Mary said, "Behold the maidservant of the Lord! Let it be to me according to your word." And the angel departed from her.

Mary believed she didn't mix belief and unbelief together. That's all you have to do to become good ground. If a young girl, who was probably petrified by the angelic visitation and scared beyond our imagination can obey under pressure, so can you.

⚿ Good ground is a simple process to the farmer and should be for the believer.

We allow the paralysis of over analysis to paralyze us when it comes to the spiritual issues. The enemy is highly developed in bringing up suggestions to keep you from acting on what you know to do. The Bible tells us to *"put on the whole armor of God that you may be able to stand against the wiles of the devil"* (Ephesians 6:11).

Satan has these plots, plans and schemes to try and confuse or cripple you from action. Let's read James 2:17 in both the New King James and the Amplified Bible. The New King James translation reads, *"Thus also faith by itself, if it does not have works, is dead."* The Amplified version says, *"So also faith, if it does not have works (deeds and actions of obedience to back it up), by itself is destitute of power (inoperative, dead)."*

⚿ You are good ground when you maintain the "Soil" of your heart.

In 1 Thessalonians 5:23, we are told, *"Now may the God of peace Himself sanctify you completely; and may your whole spirit, soul, and body be preserved blameless at the coming of our Lord Jesus Christ."* Paul teaches us that we are spirit, soul and body, and each must be controlled and tended to much as a farmer tends his land. You are a tri-part being and all three need attention and maintenance if you're going to receive the harvest in life that you dream about.

Spirit

⚿ Your spirit is the real you, the part of you that is eternal.

If you are born again, your spirit is alive unto God. But in most cultures, and especially our Western culture, the spirit is the least developed part of our being. Some spend thousands on plastic surgery to improve and accessorize their bodies. (And you should go ahead and do so, if you want to. Thank God we have options in this country. If your nose has a bump and you don't like it, you can change it and more power to you.) We can choose food, and spend hundreds of dollars a year on gym memberships. You name it; we can get it and use it to make our bodies' look and feel better. But the body isn't going to last forever, no matter how well we treat it. We sow much attention to our bodies, some attention to our souls, and almost none to the part of us that lives throughout eternity.

By trusting Christ's death, burial and resurrection, you can confess Him as Lord and be born again. That belief and confession causes your spirit to be reborn and live eternally. But we spend comparatively little time, effort and resources to develop and become more sensitive to our new life in Christ. Consider that you are a spirit, you have a soul, and you live in a body. If you begin to give more attention to spiritual things, you can develop an aptitude for them. I'm talking about controlling the issues of life so you can be good ground in every area.

You can choose to abide in Him and His Word to abide and live in you. Then you can bear fruit. John 8:31-32 reads, *Then Jesus said to those Jews who believed in Him, "If you abide in My word, you are My disciples indeed. And you shall know the truth, and the truth shall make you free."* When you continue in His Word, you'll know the truth. He's given you the key to controlling your life and bearing fruit. You must attend to His Word in order to know the truth.

We sometimes see people who have developed sensitivity or an aptitude toward spiritual things, and because they are so rare we call them fanatics, strange and extreme. But, when we see people highly developed in sports; folks who put on team jerseys, wave pom-poms, and paint their faces in team colors; we call them fans, not fanatics.

All of us get little twinges and evidences of the spirit realm, so we might as well deal with it. Have you ever had thoughts, intuitions or perception about something as simple as knowing the phone is about to ring and then it does? Or someone you haven't seen in years is suddenly on your mind, and then you bump into them in an airport somewhere. Maybe you get a card with an encouraging word from a friend at just the right time. Traces of the spirit life are evident in little events like that. You can cultivate the good ground and become more aware of the spiritual side of life. You can grow from having little twinges and experiences to a point where you are led by the Spirit of God. Consider Galatians 5:16-17 & 25,

> *"I say then: Walk in the Spirit, and you shall not fulfill the lust of the flesh. For the flesh lusts against the Spirit, and the Spirit against the flesh; and these are contrary to one another, so that you do not do the things that you wish....If we live in the Spirit, let us also walk in the Spirit."*

Here's the sixty-four thousand dollar question: What is walking in the Spirit? The following Scriptures explain:

> *"It is the Spirit who gives life; the flesh profits nothing. The words that I speak to you are spirit, and they are life."* (John 6:63)

> *"All Scripture is given by inspiration of God, and is profitable for doctrine, for reproof, for correction, for instruction in righteousness, that the man of God may be complete, thoroughly equipped for every good work."* (2 Timothy 3:16-17)

I've studied the Bible from cover to cover, and walking in the Spirit is not weird. I think people who take the truths in the Bible and get weird are just weird people. If you do a little research, you'll probably notice that they were strange before they ever started reading the Bible. Spending time in

God's Word is the foundation to walking in the Spirit. If you don't know God's language, how will you know that it's Him when He speaks to you?

Soul

The soul is made up of five parts: mind, emotion, will, intellect and imagination. Getting a good harvest in all of these areas means you must cultivate your soul. You have to grow, mature and develop in your mind. I know I've grown in my soul, because twenty years ago, I'd get road rage, even when people weren't driving fast enough. Once, I was running late and had to make up time and people just weren't co-operating by hurrying themselves along. I used to let things like that affect my whole being, but I've grown. Now I just start out five minutes earlier, and I can relax, no matter how slow I have to go. That didn't happen overnight, it took sometime, and I was a slow learner.

> ✐ **You can cultivate your soul and use your mind to think about productive things.**

Emotionally, you have to grow beyond the things that would send you into a tailspin. Imagine things working out for your benefit. You can cultivate your will and learn to resist that second piece of pie. You can grow intellectually through good books, seminars or whatever profitable materials stretch the gray matter.

> ✐ **Good ground isn't a matter of chance, but choice.**

Body

This is the part to which we give particular attention, time and money. The spirit of man only periodically gets attention. Maybe we go to Church once in a while or listen or watch a spiritual program on radio or TV or the internet. Many people really don't focus on growing and cultivating themselves spiritually. Obviously, you're reading this book to improve yourself, so you're already a part of the 10% of people who will do what it takes. The other 90% of people stuff themselves with the nightly news, American Idol, sports TV, online poker, etc. Things like that really don't challenge us; they delude and entertain us. We'll go to great lengths to cultivate the body. We've talked some about this already, but it's important to remember that the body gets most of the attention. If it's hungry, we feed it. If it's cold, we cover it. If it's uncomfortable, we attend to its every need.

My son, give attention to my words; incline your ear to my sayings. (Proverbs 4:20)

The Bible tells us to attend to God's Word first. The body and its desires can never be satisfied; they must eventually be denied. Controlling your body and its appetites will definitely keep the flesh from controlling you and stopping you from God's best. A lack of control can be a stumbling block and a hindrance to a better tomorrow.

We'll talk about controlling our environment in detail in the next chapter. A farmer grows tomato plants in a greenhouse to protect the young susceptible plants from the elements. Like him, you must have control over the Spirit, Soul and Body. It will determine your victory or your failure.

Chapter 10
Controlling Your Environment

Most good farmers try their best to control all the variables that might affect their fields and eventually their harvest. They can plow, dig, disk and irrigate, so they do. They can fertilize to increase yield, so they do. They can use pesticides to control the harvest stealers, so they do. Greenhouses are used to control the environment so that young plants can get a good start before their planting. Farmers and ranchers also use fences to establish boundaries, to keep some things in and other things out of their fields.

If you and I are going to have fertile ground to bring forth a harvest, then our environments must be controlled.

✁ We must have clearly defined boundaries protecting our hearts.

Jesus established this principle clearly in Mark 4:24-25,
Then He said to them, 'Take heed what you hear. With the same measure you use, it will be measured to you; and to you who hear, more will be given. For whoever has, to him more will be given; but whoever does not have, even what he has will be taken away from him."

The same verse in the Amplified Bible reads,
And He said to them, "Be careful what you are hearing. The measure [of thought and study] you give [to the truth you hear] will be the measure [of virtue and knowledge] that comes back to you – and more [besides] will be given to you who hear. For to him who has, more will be given; and from him who has nothing, even what he has will be taken away [by force]."

Jesus set up several boundaries in the parable of the sower.

He warned us to be careful of what we hear, a statement which seems rather innocuous. If you are not discerning, you'll have already read right over the top of that last sentence and not really thought it through. There are so many voices out in this world, and all of them are trying to be heard. Turn on the nightly news and get a dose of drama, accidents, murder, and violence. There are so many voices. But the Lord took the time to get our attention and say: 'Be careful what you are hearing.' In other words, many other boundaries can be found to help us get the best harvest possible.

🔑 Think about what you think about.

I taught a series of messages back in the mid-nineties on that very subject. You have to slow down long enough to deliberately process what you're thinking and why you're thinking it. Where do the thoughts come from? Is each one worth thinking? And what future thoughts and actions will this thinking lead me to? There are some thoughts that don't originate from God, and there are some that definitely originate in Hell. If you are to remain good ground, you have to ask yourself, "Where are my thoughts coming from?" Control your mental and emotional environment.

Each of us has been given the ability to choose, and God has challenged His people to choose rightly. In the following verses, God shows us what thoughts to entertain and what thoughts to reject:

"Finally, brethren, whatever things are true, whatever things are noble, whatever things are just, whatever things are pure, whatever things are lovely, whatever things are of good report, if there is any virtue and if there is anything praiseworthy— meditate on these things." (Philippians 4:8)

"Do not envy the oppressor, and choose none of his ways." (Proverbs 3:31)

"Now, therefore, fear the LORD, serve Him in

sincerity and in truth, and put away the gods which your fathers served on the other side of the River and in Egypt. Serve the LORD! And if it seems evil to you to serve the LORD, choose for yourselves this day whom you will serve, whether the gods which your fathers served that were on the other side of the River, or the gods of the Amorites, in whose land you dwell. But as for me and my house, we will serve the LORD." (Joshua 24:14-15)

Joshua challenged Israel to choose who they would serve. We have to have boundaries in our life when it comes to our thoughts. This is one of the most crucial ways of controlling our environment. Control your thinking. You might say, "Why is this subject of thinking so important, and is it really tied so closely to our environments and having a great harvest?' I'm glad you asked. Proverbs 23:7 says, *"For as he thinks in his heart, so is he."* Take a moment to really understand this concept: as a man thinks in his heart, so is he.

What are your thoughts, those deep thoughts, those same fears and worries or fantasies that repeat over and over again? We think thousands of thoughts a day; we might as well choose to be in control of our thoughts because they're controlling us! (See Colossians 3:1-4.)

⚿ Today you are the product and sum total of what you have been thinking about.

Your beliefs are a product of what you have received as truth. The words we hear and then think about have the power of death and life.

My wife and I were recently in New Jersey speaking at a great church. We met a lovely lady at a restaurant who was from Nigeria. You might remember her from Chapter 8. She'd been in America for twenty years with her daughter and no husband. She told us her daughter would soon graduate from medical school in New York. How did this woman do it? How did she move from Africa across the world to a foreign country and put her daughter through school on an average wage without the help of the government or a husband? I'll tell you how, she thought it was possible, and then she kept acting on it every day. My question to you is what's your excuse? Are you using your education, location, color, background, gender or financial position as an excuse? I've heard it said that excuses are the crutches for the uncommitted. This lady from Nigeria was like that little engine that could. "I think I can. I think I can."

Well, Paul agrees! He says in Philippians 4:13, *"I can do all things through Christ who strengthens me."* There's a saying I've had for the last twenty five years:

🔑 Those who say they can, and those who say they can't are both right.

I want to talk you out of not trying. I look in the Bible, see those great promises and ask, "Who are these promises not for?" The answer is that they are for whosoever will believe. God is not a respecter of persons, and His promises are good, whether you're an "up and outer" or a "downtowner", from the uttermost to the guttermost.

Clearly defined boundaries are what separates one farmer's field from another, and clearly defined boundaries in your mind establish what is acceptable and what's not. Remember Philippians 4:8 and think on those things. That's a boundary. Think on the things that will propel you onward and upward. Set boundaries around your mind and recognize that those boundaries keep certain things in your mind and certain things out of your mind and helps control our environments.

I love how Philippians 4:8 ends with a command to think on or meditate on those things which have virtue. Then a little bit further on in Philippians Chapter 4, verse 13 encourages us that we can do all things through Christ.

Wrap your mind around that principle for a while. At first it will make your brain hurt, but after a while it will become an established boundary. You will not cower away from trying circumstances if you believe you can do all things. In fact, the Bible calls you a doer of the Word. In Philippians 4:19, Paul gives us more encouragement: *"And my God shall supply all your need according to His riches in glory by Christ Jesus."* 1 John 4:4 reminds us, *"You are of God, little children, and have overcome them, because He who is in you is greater than he who is in the world."*

Many of us need to establish a new set of boundaries in our thinking. If you've failed in business, marriage, morals or spirituality, it's time to establish a new set of boundaries in your mind. If we fail, we fail in the mind first! Proverbs 23:7, *"For as he thinks in his heart, so is he."*

✐ Never allow the failures of the past create a new culture of failure for your future.

You can change your future by your thoughts, words and actions. Focus is a powerful ally for the believer. It's a key to controlling your environment. When we focus on the hidden mysteries, we can discover the truth hidden for us. Philippians 3:12 tells us, *"Not that I have already attained, or am already perfected; but I press on, that I may lay hold of that for which Christ Jesus has also laid hold of me."*

A laser is focused light, and it's powerful. You have the light of the Word living on the inside of you. What do you think would happen when we focus on that?

I heard a story twenty-four years ago at a Jerry Savelle meeting, about a lion tamer who went into a cage at the circus every day with lions and tigers to perform his act. He took three things with him: a gun full of blanks, a whip and a chair. The lion tamer was asked if he could only have one of those items, which would it be? His answer was surprising. He'd take the chair, because the lions and tigers naturally focus on the closest object to them. As the lion tamer waved the chair in front of them, the four legs protruding from the bottom of the chair had an almost hypnotic effect. The animals tried to focus on four things at the same time. This lack of focus made the lions and tigers docile and easy to work with.

Too many times, we focus on things that have no eternal value which can cause us to lose focus. We all have little annoyances spring up each day. We don't have to allow them to dominate our thinking When we concentrate on the unimportant it can drain our passion and power.

Another crucial step in controlling your personal environment is focusing on what you know the will of God is for your life with your imagination. Don't turn me off and think I just went off the deep end of the pool. Your imagination is part of your soul. It's God given and scriptural for you to use your imagination to control your mental and emotional environment. All of us are already doing it. So we might as well use our imagination correctly.

In Genesis 11:1-8 we see that anything they could imagine, they could accomplish. I won't go into great detail here because this is the subject of an upcoming book. But let's realize we all use our imagination every day. Some for the positive while others for the very destructive. Ephesians 4:17-18,

> *"This I say, therefore, and testify in the Lord,*
> *that you should no longer walk as the rest of the*
> *Gentiles walk, in the futility of their mind, having*
> *their understanding darkened, being alienated from*
> *the life of God, because of the ignorance that is in*
> *them, because of the blindness of their heart;"*

Paul told us not to be like the gentiles. They have their understanding darkened. The word understanding is the same word translated in other places for imagination. The meaning is deep thoughts. So these gentiles had empty minds filled with perverseness. These imaginations or deep thoughts were empty and clouded. They did not have God or His promises as part of their deep thinking. As we see in verses 19 and 20, these negative perverse empty deep thoughts grow from thoughts to beyond feelings. Really they become strongholds or compunctions. In verse 20, Paul tells the church at Ephesus that they didn't learn that thinking process from Christ. Our imagination should be a tool that keeps us motivated and engaged in the process. As Pastor Cho in South Korea says, "We can visit our future on the canvas of our imagination."

Think on this scripture: Hebrews 11:1, *"Now faith is the substance of things hoped for, the evidence of things not seen."* Faith is the proof or title deed. What is hope after all? Isn't it a mechanism of the mind that allows us to dream, speculate, and imagine the outcome of our faith! The Amplified version says it this way,

"NOW FAITH is the assurance (the confirmation, the title deed) of the things [we] hope for, being the proof of things [we] do not see and the conviction of their reality [faith perceiving as real fact what is not revealed to the senses]."

Philippians 4:8, *"Finally, brethren, whatever things are true, whatever things are noble, whatever things are just, whatever things are pure, whatever things are lovely, whatever things are of good report, if there is any virtue and if there is anything praiseworthy—meditate on these things."*

Meditate on these things. In other words, think about what you're thinking about. Visualizing the outcome of God's Word and prayer should be part of the process. We already do this in the negative. It's called worry and anxiety. All we have to do is reverse the worry and see, imagine, dream, and visualize the positive outcome of God's promises. This is controlling our mental environment. Hebrews 12:2,

"looking unto Jesus, the author and finisher of our faith, who for the joy that was set before Him

endured the cross, despising the shame, and has sat down at the right hand of the throne of God."

Proverbs 29:18 (King James Version), *"Where there is no vision, the people perish: but he that keepeth the law, happy is he.*

If there is no direction, dream, goal or image; you are just chasing shadows.

Each New Year's Eve people make resolutions. That's just a dream or vision you want to come to pass. We should flood our personal environment with reminders of our resolutions, goals and dreams. If we don't write down our New Year's resolutions or goals and dreams, we will forget them and never chase them. Like the majority of people who never look at their resolutions all year and eventually forget them and therefore never achieve them. The dreams die. Haven't you ever heard the saying, "out of sight, out of mind?"

Habakkuk 2:2-4, *Then the LORD answered me and said: "Write the vision And make it plain on tablets, That he may run who reads it. For the vision is yet for an appointed time; But at the end it will speak, and it will not lie. Though it tarries, wait for it; Because it will surely come, It will not tarry. Behold the proud, His soul is not upright in him; But the just shall live by his faith."*

Write it down, look at your goal as you're running to it! Looking at your dreams with external props such as written goals, pictures and proclamations that will inspire you, keeps you engaged in the process. Jesus said to be careful what you see and hear because it has an effect. Remember your uplook affects your outlook. (See Mark 4:24.)

Boundaries that control our environments are evident in several parables to help us in establishing priorities and values. Jesus said in Mark 4:21, *"Is a lamp brought to be put under a basket or under a bed? Is it not to be set on a lampstand?"* No, of course, a lamp isn't brought to be placed under a basket or under a bed. In those two locations, you would be defeating the purpose of light. The obvious answer to the question is to put the lamp in a prominent place and take advantage of what the lamp was designed to do. The Word isn't supposed to be hidden in monasteries away from the people. No, let the Word have its prominent place, not hidden, but revealed to all who need the light.

Four verses later in Mark 4:25, Jesus gives us a choice of two consequences, *"For whoever has, to him more will be given; but whoever does not have, even what he has will be taken away from him."* If you have the Word, and it is a predominant priority in your life, more revelation will be given to you. But if you don't make the Word the priority, Satan will come to steal away all of it. This is a clearly defined boundary. The Word is life to those of us who find it and health to all our flesh.

In Mark 4:26-29,

And He [Jesus] said, 'The kingdom of God is as if a man should scatter seed on the ground, and should sleep by night and rise by day, and the seed should sprout and grow, he himself does not know how. For the earth yields crops by itself: first the blade, then the head, after that the full grain in the head. But when the grain ripens, immediately he puts in the sickle, because the harvest has come."

These verses teach us the value of a process. Jesus makes it clear that you don't have to know everything to get a crop growing. If you'll just be faithful in the Word and put it in fertile ground, it will grow. You might not see progress, but believe me, if you're good ground, others will see your development.

Here's another key to understanding the process so you won't get discouraged or frustrated. The earth yields by itself, first the blade, then the ear, then the full grain in the head and then the harvest. Do you see the progression and process? Of course, Satan will use some of this against you. He'll try and beat your brains in so that you don't know exactly how this harvest is coming. Here's the good news, you don't have to know. Kenneth Copeland puts it this way, "Faith deals with the unseen not the unknown."

⚷ Just continue sleeping by night and rising by day and keep steady progress.

God will give the increase. Mark 4:28-29 reads,
"For the earth yields crops by itself: first the blade, then the head, after that the full grain in the head. But when the grain ripens, immediately he puts in the sickle, because the harvest has come."

If you're a quitter, just make a commitment to get started in the Kingdom of God and give yourself a break. Be patient. Don't let the devil discourage you about slow growth. Slow growth is good growth. Remind yourself often that Christianity is not a hundred yard dash, but a marathon. This mentality will help keep the environment of your thinking grounded. Discouragement is a lie from the devil. He'll attempt to get you to look at your field, and then compare it to your neighbor's field. That's a trap. Run your race; get your prize, like Paul told us to in Philippians 3:14: *"I press toward the goal for the prize of the upward call of God in Christ Jesus."*

The process is to start small and grow. If you've never owned a home, don't try and get a million dollar home as your first one! Start where you're at. Believe for an entry level home and be faithful with that. God will reward your faithfulness. I've known pastors who won't stay planted in their city. If their church hasn't grown to hundreds in the first year, they look for another town. I can think of a few who never seem to get settled anywhere. I know a brother who had a good church here in my county. He was doing well and making an impact. But he got frustrated in the process. He wanted to start with the blade, skip all the other steps, and go right to the harvest. He's been bumping around for 10 years now without getting planted anywhere. It's very important to control the environment of our thinking and expectations.

Remember in school, the teachers would give information for several days and then one day you walked in and things changed? The teacher said, "Put your books away and take out a pencil for a pop quiz." That's what happens to us too. Once we get some information, here comes the test. It never comes when we want it to. It's like old Gomer Pyle said, 'Surprise, Surprise, Surprise.' Keep a good environment of the Word so you'll pass every test and trial.

The disciples were tested in Mark 4:35-41,

> On the same day, when evening had come, He said to them, "Let us cross over to the other side." Now when they had left the multitude, they took him along in the boat as He was. And other little boats were also with Him. And a great windstorm arose, and the waves beat into the boat, so that it was already filling. But He was in the stern, asleep on a pillow. And they awoke Him and said to Him, 'Teacher, do You not care that we are perishing?" Then He arose and rebuked the wind, and said to the sea, "Peace, be still!" And the wind ceased and there was a great calm. But He said to them, "Why are you so fearful? How is it that you have no faith?" And they feared exceedingly, and said to one another, "Who can this be, that even the wind and the sea obey Him"

They heard the words from Jesus, "Let us cross over to the other side," and before they can accomplish His will, a storm began to blow. Isn't this exactly what happens to us? We hear the Word, and out of nowhere there comes a storm of hurricane proportions. When the pressure was on, they forgot what Jesus taught them. Keep a good environment. Remember when storms come up; don't let the storm inside your boat.

🔑 Fear got the better of them because they were not looking at the Word, but at the circumstances.

What was their reaction in verse 38? "Do you not care that we're perishing?" Listen, Jesus is in the boat with you! You're going to make it even if you have to walk on water! I've never seen the righteous forsaken. (Psalm 37:25)

Human nature is so predicable. It's a good thing that Jesus is in all of our boats. I've become irrational and lost it just like the disciples. Fear overtook them and paralyzed their faith. Faith is believing, speaking and acting. In 2 Corinthians 4:13, Paul reminds us, *"And since we have the same spirit of faith, according to what is written, 'I believed and therefore I spoke, we also believe and therefore speak."* The disciples blew it. Any one of them could have stepped up and encouraged the others not to be afraid. They could have been the ones to take authority and say, "Peace be still" to the storm. You can too! Your life can get pretty stormy, but you can be the one that speaks God's Word in the face of the wind and the waves. You don't have to let the stones and thorns choke the Word. You control your environment and heart.

Let's look at Matthew 14:22-33 to see what happened the next time the disciples were in a storm together.

Immediately, Jesus made His disciples get into the boat and go before Him to the other side, while He sent the multitudes away. And when He had sent the multitudes away, He went up on the mountain by Himself to pray. Now when evening came, He was alone there. But the boat was now in the middle of the sea, tossed by the waves, for the wind was contrary. Now in the fourth watch of the night Jesus went to them, walking on the sea. And when the disciples saw Him walking on the sea, they were troubled, saying, "It is a ghost!" And they cried out for fear. But immediately Jesus spoke to them, saying, "Be of good cheer! It is I; do not be afraid." And Peter answered Him and said, "Lord, if it is You, command me to come to You on the water." So He said, "Come." And when Peter had come down out of the boat, he walked on the water to go to Jesus. But when he saw that the wind was boisterous, he was afraid; and beginning to sink, he cried out, saying, "Lord, save me!" And immediately, Jesus stretched out His hand and caught him, and said to him, "O you of little faith, why did you doubt?" And when they got into the boat, the wind ceased. Then those who were in the boat came and worshipped him, saying, "Truly You are the Son of God."

It has been said that Peter wasn't walking on the water, but walking on the Word. When Jesus said, "Come," he stepped out of the boat onto the Word. It's only when you get your eyes off the Word and onto the storm that you begin to sink. Once you receive the Word from the Lord on any subject you know that a storm of some kind will try to separate you from your God given promises, whether they're for healing, prosperity, favor, or peace of mind. The enemy attacks our environment with circumstances because he can manipulate this natural realm.

The enemy is a liar and will try to get you to look at anything other than the Word. He'll use cares, persecutions, tribulations – anything to get you to focus on the problems and not what the Lord said. You can control your environment. (See Colossians 3:15-16.)

⚷ You can control what you see and what you hear even in the middle of the storm, if you keep your eyes on Him.

Chapter 11
Preparing for the Harvest

Preparation is vital. To prepare means to do something beforehand. *Pre*-pare. It's not the will to win; it's the will to prepare to win. Matthew 12:33-37 tells us,

"Either make the tree good and its fruit good, or else make the tree bad and its fruit bad; for a tree is known by its fruit...For by your words you will be justified, and by your words you will be condemned."

You either will make the tree good and its fruit good or you won't. You have a choice. Make it good or bad by preparing or not preparing. Jesus prepared the disciples for a boat trip and all the contingencies that might arise. Even though He prepared them, they forgot under pressure. Pressure exposes us. Every person is like a tube of toothpaste. As long as you leave the cap on, you can apply a little pressure and the contents of the tube will remain unknown. Remove the cap and put some pressure on the tube and you'll see what's inside.

In Mark 4:35, Jesus told the disciples his will and plan. Jesus said, *"Let us cross over to the other side."* That was His will. Jesus' will was not for them to drown in a storm halfway across the water. What's amazing is that when you see a Bible truth and you place your faith in God and His Word, the enemy will rise up to resist you and attempt to discourage you. Storms are the vehicles the devil uses to get your focus away from going to the other side. The devil wants to create circumstances that lead you to reason yourself out of ever getting across. At the first sign of the storm, the enemy will start talking to you: "You should never have left the safety of the shore; you're going to drown." That's a lie in itself, because rain and lightening happen onshore too. If those thoughts are not interrupted and contradicted, your mind will have you doubting whether you should have ever left the shore in obedience to God. The waves and thunder and lightening all influence your senses, and pretty soon you're conceding defeat in your soul.

This story is played out every time the Word of God is challenged by this natural world, which is under the control of Satan. I must resist the devil in this realm, *"...casting down arguments and every high thing that exalts itself against the knowledge of God, bringing every though into captivity to the obedience of Christ."* (2 Corinthians 10:5) I must stand on God's Word during trials.

The enemy will not stop his deceptions until we take authority over him. He's a bully who will pick on the sick, the weak, and the ignorant. That's what a bully does.

(See Mark 4:35-41 and John 6:15-21.) As Jesus rebuked the wind and the waves, the boat arrived on the opposite shore, and the disciples were still trying to figure out who this Jesus was. Even the wind and waves obeyed Him. He was the same Jesus who said, "Let us cross over to the other side." He's the same Jesus who rebuked them, and basically said, "Why didn't you use your faith and speak to the wind and waves yourself?" He taught them this back in Mark 11:22-24. If they had planted Jesus' commands in a heart with good ground, they would have come through the storm by themselves, without ever having to wake Jesus.

⚷ With God, you always get another chance to overcome. You always get another chance to pass the tests of life.

The next Scripture starts another test to see if the disciples had really learned from the last test. A lot of what we call tests are just opportunities to prepare for our harvest. Mark 5:1-8 reads,

Then they came to the other side of the sea, to the country of the Gadarenes. And when He had come

126

out of the boat, immediately there met Him out of
the tombs a man with an unclean spirit, who had his
dwelling among the tombs; and no one could bind
him, not even with chains, because he had been often
bound with shackles and chains. And the chains had
been pulled apart by him, and the shackles broken in
pieces; neither could anyone tame him. And always,
night and day, he was in the mountains and in the
tombs, crying out and cutting himself with stones.
When he saw Jesus from afar, he ran and worshipped
Him. And he cried out with a loud voice and said,
"What have I to do with You, Jesus, Son of the Most
High God? I implore You by God that You do not
torment me." For He said to him, "Come out of this
man, unclean spirit!"

I love the Bible. It shows us exactly where we live and how
we operate in our strengths and weaknesses. First the disciples
had to wake Jesus up to save themselves from drowning, and
then they were immediately faced with another type of test.
The demoniac was fierce, shackled, and strong. He was so
violent, he even cut himself. As soon as the disciples walked
off the boat, he got right in their faces. Jesus again had to
take authority, this time over the demoniac. It's a good thing
the disciples had Jesus with them, or, in the course of one day,
they would have either been drowned or killed by a demon
possessed man. Sound familiar?

Once Jesus rose from the dead, and the disciples were
filled with the Holy Spirit, they started taking control of the
situations they found themselves facing. Acts 3:1-10 shows
us how far they had come,

Now Peter and John went up together to the
temple at the hour of prayer, the ninth hour. And
a certain man lame from his mother's womb was
carried, whom they laid daily at the gate of the temple
which is called Beautiful, to ask alms from those who

entered the temple; who, seeing Peter and John about to go into the temple, asked for alms. And fixing his eyes on him, with John, Peter said, "Look at us." So he gave them his attention, expecting to receive something from them. Then Peter said, "Silver and gold I do not have, but what I do have I give you: in the name of Jesus Christ of Nazareth, rise up and walk." And he took him by the right hand and lifted him up, and immediately his feet and ankle bones received strength. So he, leaping up, stood and walked and entered the temple with them—walking, leaping, and praising God.

Wow! Just a short time before, they would have freaked out and depended on Jesus to deliver them. 'Jesus, come over here and heal this man, he really needs your help!' They would have been filled with fear and paralyzed by circumstances. But now they were taking authority. They were in control, and could not be intimidated by the devil. Why? Because they knew and understood the key to the parable.

🔑 The heart must be dominated by the Word. In order to have a harvest we must be dominated by God's Word.

Unbelief, questions and doubt must be managed while you apply God's Word. Once you know this principle, you'll learn that you can continue to manage your fears until you see fruit born out of any circumstance.

In Acts Chapter 16, Paul and Silas were thrown into prison. They didn't deserve their punishment because they weren't in sin. Even if they had been in sin, God would not have put them in prison. They had simply been preaching the Gospel in obedience to God's Word. While they were preaching, enemies to the Gospel were stirred up by Satan to get them off the Word of God. A girl had been possessed with a spirit of divination. She was a fortune teller and she made a lot of money for her employers. She had become a nuisance to Paul constantly crying after them that they were men of God. Paul got fed up with it and he commanded the spirit out of her. Satan used these enemies of the Gospel to incite a riot among the people causing Paul and Silas to be thrown into prison.

Pay close attention to their response to their situation in verses 25-32,

> But at midnight Paul and Silas were praying and singing hymns to God, and the prisoners were listening to them. Suddenly there was a great earthquake, so that the foundations of the prison were shaken; and immediately all the doors were opened and everyone's chains were loosed.

Paul and Silas could have cried and moaned and groaned about their troubles. They would have been like people I know who question God about their circumstances. "God, all we were doing was obeying you. Why did this happen to us? Now we're in jail...." When things are bad, some people go negative and they go on and on and on. Paul and Silas didn't choose that way. Instead, they sang praises to God. They had sown the Word into a heart of good ground and produced a harvest of freedom.   This is a principle that's found in both the New and the Old Testament.

Faith, belief and confidence in God or assurance are big issues in spiritual matters. Hebrews 10:35-36 in the Amplified version tells us,

> "Do not, therefore, fling away your fearless confidence, for it carries a great and glorious compensation of reward. For you have need of steadfast patience and endurance, so that you may perform and fully accomplish the will of God, and thus receive and carry away [and enjoy to the full] what is promised."

The farmer has confidence in the coming harvest because

he has been preparing and because he has seen the process year after year.

If you're expecting a harvest of healing, favor, blessing, and prosperity. Then,

🔑 You should have confidence because it's God who told us not to cast away our confidence.

God has shown us all His ability to move in situations that seemed impossible in our lives and the lives of others. My pastor tells the story of the church's first building. It was a huge step of faith They had believed for months for the $50,000 needed for closing to come. Months went by and they kept believing. In the morning, a few hours before the closing, someone walked into the church with a $50,000 check to take to the closing table.

I vividly remember the morning of September 11, 2001. Our nation was under attack. We all can remember that day. I drove to one school and Joselyn to another to pick up the two younger children. As I was picking up my son David, I got a call from my oldest daughter in Denver. She was afraid just as we all were. She didn't know if this was World War III. She knew how much I fly in and out of the northeast and didn't know where I was. She was unsaved and full of fear. That day as I had just picked up David, I got to pray the prayer of salvation with my daughter 1,500 miles away. To say the least, we were both crying and very emotional. As I got off the phone with Emy, David said, "Dad, I was praying right with you as Emy gave her heart to Christ." David was six years old.

God is still in the miracle business today. Something good can come from something bad. You may be in a real bad spot today but God's got you covered.

We've seen God answer prayers in the past. We've heard the testimony of others, how God blessed them even when it looked hopeless. Even more than that, we have God's own

Word, so we don't have to wad up our confidence and throw it away. I'm glad that I know people who have gone before me and have seen God move in tremendous ways. But we also have God's Word and that settles all questions. That gives me the greatest confidence, because, *"Jesus Christ is the same yesterday, today, and forever."* (Hebrews 13:8) God's Word gives us a more sure foundation than any testimony or story. Your harvest is too important to build on an unstable foundation. So build on the written Word of God. Let's prepare for the harvest.

Let's take a little time to read about incredible harvests that have been recorded in the Bible. In Numbers Chapter 13 Moses sends spies into the land of Canaan to scout out the land,

> *And the Lord spoke to Moses, saying, "Send men to spy out the land of Canaan, which I am giving to the children of Israel; from each tribe of their fathers you shall send a man, every one a leader among them...Then Moses sent them to spy out the land of Canaan..."*

The rest of the Chapter talks about how 10 out of the 12 spies brought back an evil report of the land. They said it couldn't be conquered because there were giants. They saw themselves like grasshoppers. They even went so far as to say that the land devoured its people. Well, if that were so, how come there were still people there?

Joshua and Caleb were the only two that saw all the potential and the good place God had led them to. Joshua and Caleb did not see that the giants needed to be conquered, but that the giants were no match for their God. All 12 spies went to the same place, looked at the same things but 10 saw nothing but war, trouble, work, and obstacles. Two saw the land flowing with milk, honey and blessing; and with God's help, an adversary they could conquer. Frank Tyger, national columnist, wrote, "Your future depends on many things, but mostly on you."

Even in old age, Joshua and Caleb continued to be good ground. It is said of them that they had a different "spirit" within them. The Hebrew word for "spirit" in this text is *mind*, which tells me that they had a completely different attitude. They had a positive attitude. They were "good ground." They had chosen to believe God at His Word and not be moved by "obstacles." They saw God greater than any obstacle. You know sometimes it's easy to overlook all the good that God has for us and be consumed with the negative. Have you ever noticed people who were so consumed with the negative that they were rarely consumed with anything else? Usually there's a lot more to be thankful for than we're willing to acknowledge. John Mason wrote, "If we would think more we would thank more." Joshua and Caleb reaped a harvest of good in their life. Joshua led his people to victory, and Caleb conquered a mountain occupied by the enemy at the age of 85! A good harvest comes when we free our hearts from negativity. Negativity is never conducive to good growth.

Joshua and Caleb were good ground, free of hardness of heart, stony ground or thorny soil. They were free of unbelief and fear. They prepared beforehand. Caleb said, "Give me the mountains where the giants are." Caleb, at eighty five years old, was still up for the battle. Some of us at 50 are ready for the couch. He and Joshua weren't full of gloom and doom. Do you remember the song from that old TV show, Hee Haw? "Gloom, despair, and agony on me; Deep dark depression, excessive misery; If it weren't for bad luck, I'd have no luck at all; Gloom despair, and agony on me."

No, Joshua and Caleb were good ground, ready to produce thirty, sixty, hundredfold in their lives. They obviously kept God's Word hidden in their hearts, as indeed we are told in Numbers. See Numbers 13:25-30.)

When you're full of enthusiasm, and full of God's Word,

you look at problems differently than people with hard hearts. They see how it can't be done.

🗝 When your heart is clear of stones, thorns and hardness, you can focus on the opportunities, not the obstacles.

You begin to see things from God's perspective. Best of all, you see how all things can work out for the good of the Gospel. Romans 8:28 puts it this way, *"And we know that all things work together for good to those who love God, to those who are the called according to his purpose."* You're not afraid of challenges when God's Word is in your heart. When you're prepared, you understand Zechariah 4:6, *"'Not by might nor by power, but by My Spirit,' says the Lord of hosts."*

Proverbs 24:10 reads, *"If you faint in the day of adversity, your strength is small."* The other ten spies who were with Joshua and Caleb went negative and influenced others with their fear. When they brought back the negative report, it was a reflection on the ten, not the two. The ten saw the cup half empty. The two saw the cup overflowing. Numbers 13:31-33 says,

> *But the men who had gone up with him said, 'We are not able to go up against the people, for they are stronger then we. And they gave the children of Israel a bad report of the land which they had spied out, saying, "The land through which we have gone as spies is a land that devours its inhabitants, and all the people whom we saw in it are men of great stature. Then we saw the giants (the descendants of Anak came from the giants); and we were like grasshoppers in our own sight, and so we were in their sight."*

"We are not able…" Wow, they reasoned God right out of the equation! Hard hearts produce no fruit. There was more than one kind of giant in the land. A giant of unbelief lived in the hearts of ten of the spies. God had it with these people's unbelief. Unbelief is a choice. God wanted to destroy these people for it, but Moses interceded for them in Numbers 14.

They were spared, but never entered and enjoyed the promised land. They eventually reaped what they had sown.

> ### 🔑 The negativity those words produced in their lives caused them to wander and perish.

Joshua and Caleb said, "We know there are mountains. We know there are giants. We know we have to climb. And we know we'll have to fight. Bring it on." If you find an excuse in life, don't pick it up. Negative, defeated people see things differently than others. They have programmed their subconscious minds to resist anything that will take effort or risk. People with hard hearts, stones and thorns in them, choke the Word, and the Word becomes unfruitful. (See Mark 4:19.) Because Joshua and Caleb had a different spirit in them, they went into the Promised Land, a land flowing with milk and honey. (vs. 24 & 30) Their hearts were prepared before the battles.

Joshua 14:12 reads,

"Now, therefore, give me this mountain of which the Lord spoke in that day; for you heard in that day how the Anakim were there, and that the cities were great and fortified. It may be that the Lord will be with me, and I shall be able to drive them out as the Lord said." Yes, there are giants and mountains, but with God in the equation everything changes. He is the great equalizer.

What you're going through now is probably really tough. It would sink many people, but because you have that "can do" spirit, you'll overcome huge obstacles. And because you're prepared for the harvest, you won't sink. Remember Philippians 4:13, *"I can do all things through Christ which strengthens me."* When your heart is good ground, you learn to be victorious, even in the middle of problems. You can be victorious and rejoice. Philippians 4:4 encourages us to, *"Rejoice in the Lord always. Again I will say, rejoice!"* And 1 John 4:4 reads, *"You are of God, little children, and have overcome them, because He who is in you is greater than he who is in the world."* You and God make up the difference. *"For whatever is born of God overcomes the world. And this is the victory that has overcome the world– our faith."* (1 John 5:4)

Whatever is in your heart in abundance will be a determining factor in your harvest. You and I are in complete control over what is in our hearts. Our harvest is too valuable to leave to the status quo. As believers, we plant with purpose and maintain good ground in our hearts since we know whatever is in our hearts in abundance is going to produce a crop. Joshua and Caleb had confidence in God's plan. The other ten spies had fear and doubt and a crowd mentality. The crowd will get you in trouble. The crowd is almost always wrong.

I remember back in the mid-80's, there was a young lady wandering through a large crowd in Central Park in New York City. Now this large crowd was full of young, unruly teens. Things got out of control, and the young lady was raped several times. After investigation by the police, the young men were arrested. Several of them said that they were just caught up in the moment and did what everyone else was doing. Always remember: the crowd will get you in trouble. Be prepared and know your own core values before the pressure is on you.

I've seen soccer matches on international TV. Hoodlums will start fights in the stands, and before you know it, the crowd is fighting each other and destruction and mayhem break out. The crowd mentality is usually wrong. Hanging around the wrong people who drag you in the wrong direction will start you on the wrong path.

⚷ It's better to be alone than with the wrong people.

A man wrote a song many years ago, and one of the lyrics was, "Nothing good ever happens to me after midnight."

As smart farmers, you and I want a good harvest out of the good ground in our hearts. We get to choose who we associate with and what we receive into our hearts. As a pastor, I hear horror stories about good people hanging around with the wrong crowd. Little by little, things that used to look bad to them didn't anymore. There's a young lady in our congregation that started hanging around some people who smoked crack cocaine. You know the end of the story. Evil company corrupts good morals. (See 1 Corinthians 15:33.)

I don't hang around men who don't esteem their wives. I don't want anything getting in my heart that would be detrimental to my relationship. I want good ground to sow the good seed of the Word of God into to generate a harvest. The good news is if we are good ground, then we can be the ones that affect the crowd. Our lives and influences can be the catalyst to influence people at the office and the mall or on a night out with friends. We can help influence people for good, not evil.

⚷ Remember, out of the good treasure of your heart, you bring forth your harvest.

You'll never lack a harvest when you continually deposit good news in a good heart. You can't help but bring forth a good harvest. Let's finish this book by talking about what the farmer does with the harvest (Matthew 12:33-35).

Chapter 12
The Harvest

The key to your harvest is good seed. Good seed that is planted in good ground, which has been cleared of hardness, stones, thorns and thistles. There is life in the Word. Put your seed in optimal soil to get the hundredfold return. Easy, right? Yes, except there's a devil, a *"The thief does not come except to steal, and to kill, and to destroy. I have come that they may have life, and that they may have it more abundantly."* (John 10:10) The culture we all live in is not conducive to bringing in bumper crops or hundredfold harvests. Remember, whatever we give our attention to causes us to have a desire for it.

"If then you were raised with Christ, seek those things which are above, where Christ is, sitting at the right hand of God. Set your mind on things above, not on things on the earth. For you died, and you life is hidden with Christ in God." (Colossians 3:1-3). *"...and that He is a rewarder of those who diligently seek Him."* (Hebrews 11:6) Those verses are the foundation for your harvest.

⚿ There's an enemy that wants to divert your attention from the Word of God.

He never wants you to understand who you are in Christ.

This process of seeking the things above and setting your mind on things above helps you realize that you have died and are positionally in Christ. If you have produced a crop of peace, joy, favor, abundance and health in your life, I know you're a product of the good thoughts you have sown into your mind. Understanding Jesus has already purchased this life for you and it is by faith you receive it (See Ephesians 1:3.). Don't mix this process up. Don't allow the enemy to deceive you into thinking negative destructive thoughts. Jesus told us to be careful what you see and hear. Proverbs 6:2 says, *"You are snared by the words of your mouth; you are taken by the words of your mouth."* The key here is to sow good seed. Let's look at two passages from the Bible:

Another parable He put forth to them, saying: "The kingdom of heaven is like a man who sowed good seed in his field; but while men slept, his enemy came and sowed tares among the wheat and went his way." (Matthew 13:24-25)

These verses say that when they slept, an enemy came and sowed tares among the good seed. The reference to sleep here could be a loss of focus, priorities or passion (enthusiasm). The thief comes in many shapes and sizes. Deception is his expertise.

Harvest time is a lot of hard work. It's a time when a lazy farmer might do too much sleeping. Proverbs 6:10-11 tells us, *"A little sleep, a little slumber, a little folding of the hands to sleep so shall your poverty come on you like a prowler, and your need like an armed man."* An enemy can do great damage if you lose your focus. Our enemy doesn't take time off.

Satan thrives on deception, and so his tares need to be described so you can identify them. They can come in the form of too much attention to television, hobbies, or work. Before you know it, the whole evening is gone. Unfortunately, you can find yourself investing your time and money on negative, non-productive things because of peer pressure. Regrettably, you don't even have to be seeking distractions to waste time. TV, video games and the like are fine in their place, but let's be honest; there are a lot of folks who have allowed these things to get way out of hand. I know a pastor who plays hours of online poker each week. I've had people tell me, "Pastor, I want one of the new 100 inch TVs so the programs and games are almost life-like in size." I want you to know the last thing we need is perversion, adultery, lying, and deception coming into our homes in life-size. Most of TV is a distraction.

⚷ Distractions will find you and zap your energy and focus.

I was sitting in a doctor's office a few months ago, and a song came on the house stereo; a song I hadn't heard in twenty years. But once I heard it, it was stuck in my head while sitting there and feeding my negative emotions. I had already been feeling lazy just sitting there. Maybe you've heard the song before, "You're no good, you're no good, you're no good. Baby you're no good." Sitting all alone in that doctor's office, I realized what was happening to me, and I started rooting out that bad seed, pulling it up with the Word of God.

I spoke to that song, and said, 'Jesus died for me. He's living on the inside of me. I'm filled with the Holy Spirit. God loves me, so there must be something good about me.' I couldn't afford to let the words of that song get planted in my heart and bring forth a harvest. I could just sit there and drift and let the thief steal it. I could fall asleep at the wheel while the enemy sowed bad seed. We are emotional beings, and negative emotions can make us susceptible to bad seed. I had to stop the enemy from affecting my soul and my harvest.

I saw a news report many years ago about a farmer who had planted a whole field of corn. But deep in the middle of the field, he left a piece of ground clear and came back to plant marijuana. Since it was covered on every side by corn, he thought this was a fool proof plan. No one would be in that field by the time the marijuana started growing, and the corn would block anyone's ability to see it from the road. He had it all planned out— except for the fact that the police and drug enforcement agencies had airplanes and helicopters.

So when they flew over this field, they saw beautiful corn...
and right in the middle of it was the marijuana. You know
the end of the story.

Out of the abundance of the heart the mouth speaks,
and words lead to actions. Lots of things promise they can
change your life, but the Word of God actually can change
your life! As Jesus says in Matthew 12:33, make the tree
good! You have a choice. God has given you free will and
common sense. You can choose your actions, and those things
on which you'll set your affections and attention. Make your
heart good ground. Make your seed good. Make your life
good. Choose this day who you are going to serve.

𝄔 One choice can dictate all the other choices in my life.

When I chose Jesus as my Savior, the course of my life was
automatically set in motion. But rejecting God's way brings
a variety of choices that might lead to destruction.

I received a letter from a man in jail in Fort Myers. He
was watching our program on TV and was familiar with
our teaching. I had mentioned a pastor during the broadcast
who he knew from Tulsa. In his letter, he told me that he was
only in Fort Myers for a few days before being transferred
to a state prison. He said that he'd never intended to murder
anyone; it just all began with one bad choice. He'd been a
deacon in his church, and he'd loved God, but he got off
track. At first, it seemed he was off the path in small ways,
until bad seed brought increasingly bad harvests, and it led
to murder.

As in Matthew 13:24-25, someone came and sowed bad
seed while the farmer was asleep; negative thoughts crept
into this man's life, and it led him to taking the wrong road.
The same process has happened to many of us.

So, how do we keep the bad seed from ever getting
planted in the field of our hearts? Matthew 7:15 reads,

"Beware of false prophets, who come to you in sheep's clothing, but inwardly they are ravenous wolves."

Harvest comes on purpose and you can stop bad seed from ever getting planted, by following these steps (John 10:10):

1. Make the soil good. You're not some weak worm of the dust. You've been created in the image and likeness of God, and you are somebody. Begin to renew your mind to God's will today, and you'll start the process of becoming good ground.

2. Speak scriptural and positive words. What is in abundance within you will come out of your mouth. Take a survey of your words. They're either working for you or against you. Speak words of faith and belief. Words are your life line between where you are and where you're going. (See Proverbs 18:21, I Samuel 3:19 and Jeremiah 1:6-9.)

🗝 Good deposits and bad deposits come. Deposit only good things in your heart.

3. Eliminate the tares. It's amazing how much better life is when you eliminate bad friends and meet some good ones. My Pastor, David Demola, puts it this way, "If you lay down with the dogs, you'll wake up with fleas." It's supernatural how a good deposit in the heart brings forth good things and you will also begin to bring forth fruit.

Don't undervalue these areas of life. Renew your mind, speak the Word and remember, your friends are a reflection of yourself. Choose your words and friends wisely. By your words you will be justified, or condemned. The words you speak tell on you.

🗝 We use our words as tools. Satan will try to use your own words to set the fires of hell ablaze in your life. (James 3:8-10.)

We have to choose to be vigilant by depositing the good

seed of the Word inside of us, proactively. Don't be like the farmer who sleeps, and allows his fields to be contaminated by an enemy. We must refuse to allow the enemy to come in when we're asleep and sow tares because it can cause huge problems.

In Matthew 12:34, speaking to the Pharisees, the religious people of His time, Jesus says, *"Brood of vipers! How can you, being evil, speak good things? For out of the abundance of the heart the mouth speaks."* Our seed is sown in many cases by the words that we speak and the friends that we choose. I'm cognizant of the people I choose as friends. I know like attracts like. You're never going to find a perfect friend because there are no perfect people. I encourage you to find a friend that has a vision and hope for their future. As best-selling author John Mason says, "I have found it is better to be alone than in the wrong company." You don't want to get caught up in other people's messes. I can create my own without help from others. Life will get better quicker with friends who know where they're going. A real friend will help you to your next level. They will encourage you onward and upward while challenging you, not enabling you. They will celebrate you and not merely tolerate you. The more you're around people the more you become like them, and vice versa. (See Proverbs 27:17.) We're supposed to sharpen the people closest to us. To have a friend is to be one. Sow into others' lives, it pays the best dividends. If you want a good harvest, the whole field must be planted with good seed.

Matthew 13:33 is a parable: *"Another parable he spoke to them: 'The kingdom of heaven is like leaven, which a woman took and hid in three measures of meal till it was all leavened.'"* This woman hid or mixed the yeast in all three measures of meal. In other words, the leaven mixed in all the flour thoroughly. When it is mixed, the yeast affects the flour to make it rise. In the same way, we mix the Word of God in our hearts until it affects every area of our lives.

Our whole life rises because it has been mixed through and through with the Word of God. So simple. We'll run all over the countryside attempting to find someone anointed by God to give us a touch. There is nothing wrong with that, but the same Word mixed in your heart can make you rise to another level.

🗝 Our whole life rises because it has been mixed through and through with the Word of God.

Harvest is not mystical or magical. It's a process that if followed, can bring repeated results. Power is in the Word, and it will cause you to bring forth in every area of your life. Another key is Matthew 13:44, *"Again, the kingdom of heaven is like treasure hidden in a field, which a man found and hid; and for joy over it he goes and sells all that he has and buys that field."*

The value you place on the Word determines the power of the seed and the quality of your harvest. Remember, the quality of the seed and ground in which it is planted; determines the quality of the harvest. The quality of your friends will help raise your life.

1. **Once you realize the value of the Word of God, you'll go to extreme lengths to possess the Word. It is a treasure!**

    You'll need wisdom to bring in the harvest. The world is changing daily so we'll need to keep pace with it. (See 1 Corinthians 1:19-20.) Get wisdom and get understanding. The harvest will demand focus and knowledge. Keep growing, keep learning. The old saying goes, "today a reader, tomorrow a leader." You'll sell anything to be able to acquire knowledge. You'll sacrifice whatever you have to gain revelation. Chances are, once you come to Christ, it's going to cost you dearly—sometimes friends, family and other things as well. Jesus tells us this in Matthew 10:34, *"Do not think that I came to bring peace on earth. I did not come to bring peace but a sword."*

There's definitely a dividing line that's drawn when you make a decision to follow Christ. People will get offended, and situations will arise in an attempt to make you compromise your values and commitments. The harvest is too valuable to waste in purposelessness. The last thing we want to do at harvest time is to lose focus on the important things that help bring in the harvest.

I know a young woman who used to be happy and had a heart after God. She had a husband and children and a call to serve God in full time ministry. She wanted to sing and dance and lead people to a life with Christ. But she started compromising, and giving her attention to things that hinder a bountiful harvest. I heard a great preacher some twenty-five years ago named Kenneth Copeland say something that I've never forgotten. "What you compromise to keep, you will ultimately lose." This young woman flirted with the wild side long enough for it to change her heart. I'm sure she never intended to become a prostitute or a drug addict. She never intended to leave her children or give up her rights to them. But not choosing to follow God with a daily commitment allowed a negative lifestyle to creep in instead. She also influenced others in her lifestyle. *"But every person is tempted when he is drawn away, enticed and baited by his own evil desire (lust, passions)."* (James 1:14, Amplified Bible)

⚿ What price are we willing to pay for Kingdom living?

By following these simple steps you can eliminate many potential problems. God never asked for a shallow commitment. That's why the state of the Church is where it is, because of shallow commitment. I have a friend who built a large church. One day he told me his concerns about the church. He stated, I don't even know if the majority of these people know how to pray for themselves. He said the church is a mile wide and an inch deep. Wow, being an inch deep never gets you to harvest. So keep learning and leading your life into a place of maturity with good friends, good resources for personal and spiritual growth. You will never become an inch deep and vulnerable to catastrophe.

We are meant to look to Jesus. In Luke 18:28, "...*Peter said, 'See, we have left all and followed You.*" There's no ambiguity in these statements. Too many want an antiseptic Christianity. Following Christ cost me a great deal. It will cost you too. But it cost Jesus everything. The rewards will be out of this world. These few keys to the harvest will be a sure foundation.

Can you imagine a farmer who is really committed only for the first day of the planting season? Picture it. Farmer Joe is up early Monday morning when the rooster crows. He fills the tractor with fuel, and hooks up the plow. Then he gets into the cab of the tractor, turns on the A/C and the radio...and just sits there. He never puts the tractor in gear to start plowing. Of course, that farmer went through the motions, but he'll never get a harvest. Good intentions must be mixed with diligence, hard work and excellence. Harvests don't just happen.

Farmer Joe needs other good farming friends who will help encourage and inspire him to be the best farmer he can be. Let's commit today to bringing in the harvest. It will take more than a fleeting feeling. Surround yourself with a reminder of what life will be like when the full harvest comes in. It will keep you inspired to follow a vision and have a dream. Someone once said, dreaming about it is half the fun. It will take a commitment to a vision of harvest, to get you through the tough times of life. Retired football coach, Lou Holtz said, "Show me someone who has done something worthwhile and I'll show you someone who has overcome adversity."

Your harvest will be filled with opposition and opportunity to quit. Refuse to miss your harvest by allowing temporary circumstances a predominant place in your mind.

Chapter 13
Key Number 4—The Servant

There's life in the seed, which is the Word, and that's one of the keys to the harvest. If you put the seed of the Word into the servant, a transformation occurs. (See 1 Peter 1:23, Hebrews 1:3, and John 1:14.) The seed grows. The servant's personal growth is tied to the Parable of the Sower, which Jesus says is the key to all the parables in the Bible. You can't get away from it, because it's a law.

The servant's personal growth is for the Master's benefit as well. Jesus is depending on us to search after the Word and accept it so that we can mature and be part of winning the world to Him.

As we have discussed, there are four keys to the harvest, seed, season, soil and the servant.

🗝 Servants do not belong to themselves.

They serve at the pleasure of another. We are God's children, and so we don't belong to ourselves any longer. Galatians 2:20 reads, *"I have been crucified with Christ; it is no longer I who live, but Christ lives in me; and the life which I now live in the flesh I live by faith in the Son of God."* As God's children, we're obedient to our Father and we're obligated to follow him and His desires.

If you want it to go well with you, obey God. Be quick to listen, obey and respond quickly. Don't be like the mule that needs a whip to move in the right direction. You should want to do what God wants you to do, without being competitive and without comparing yourself to others. You should be competent and conscientious. God has not called you to be a star, but to be a servant. Matthew 23:11 says, *"But he who is greatest among you shall be your servant."* Stars want to be served. We see them on TV and read about them in magazines. Many are good, functional people who have worked hard and are appreciative for their successes. They are humble and benevolent. But we've also seen others who have not adjusted well to fame, success and fortune.

I have heard a testimony recently about Oprah Winfrey. She's on a spiritual quest and is seeking. So she visited several churches, one being Lakewood Church in Houston Texas where Joel and Victoria Osteen pastor. Even though Oprah is popular and known all over the world, she arrived with just her friend. No security, no entourage, no private green rooms. It was just Oprah and her friend. Today, we have lots of servants of God that could learn from Oprah.

The servant who God is looking to use is humble. James 4:10 urges us to, *"Humble yourselves in the sight of the Lord, and He will lift you up."* Too many servants are breaking their arms patting themselves on the back. As believers who are out in the harvest field, we know that it's God who is working behind the scenes to bring increase and success. Philippians 4:13 encourages us: *"I can do all things through Christ who strengthens me..."* God won't share His glory with man. When Jesus went to Jerusalem on a colt, wouldn't it have been silly for the colt to think all the praise and attention was for him? Can you just imagine the colt saying, 'Wow, how great am I?' (See Luke 19:33-38.) No, when God uses us, it's not about the servant, but about the one who called us. God uses us not because of us, but in spite of us.

You and I have seen people who have received the slightest amount of attention or success, and allowed it to go right to their heads. Someone once said, "Power corrupts, and absolute power corrupts absolutely." If you want to know what's in someone's heart, give them power. It's a shame, but I've seen people go crazy with a little authority. I gave a man the title of Associate Pastor many years ago. One of his responsibilities was to oversee the Children's Church. But because he got a title and position, he made a new rule. No parent could drop off their children to the Children's Ministry classrooms after church started. Mr. Wonderful began to turn families away from church because they were a few minutes late, the same parents and children without whom he wouldn't have had a job or a paycheck. I don't want to foster an attitude of being late, but we live under grace not the law.

In 1 Peter 5:7 it tells of *"casting all your care upon Him, for He cares for you."* The key here is to humble yourself. Each time the Lord uses you in some way, remind yourself that it's all about God and furthering His Kingdom, not about you or your reputation. The servant must be humble to get the harvest.

A key to keeping things in perspective is through understanding the difference between the source and a resource. When we humble ourselves we begin to understand God used donkeys, fish, birds, whales, ants, flowers locusts and frogs. We need to realize that God uses us in spite of us and our little idiosyncrasies. After being a student of people for years, I've learned that we're all dysfunctional in some way. That is why we needed the Savior. That is why God sent us the Holy Spirit. *Because we're not the source, we're just a resource for the Lord.*

The farmer knows he is only a source. He cannot create seeds, soil, sunshine or rain. Only the source can do that. The farmer is just a resource we tap into when we go shopping. We are a resource God can tap into when He wants His will done on the Earth. Mankind is an essential part of the process. But, always remember, God's eyes are always going to and fro looking to use someone. (See 2 Chronicles 16:9.) There is no right way to do a prideful thing. I see frustrated prideful people failing every day. Reality shows are filled with them. It doesn't take a genius to realize our culture is creating a generation of self indulgent mega maniacs. The Bible teaches us to humble ourselves. (James 4:10). I caution you not to run in the other ditch and start a pity party thinking of yourself as some weak worm of the dust.

Moreover, the servant must be excellent. Vince Lombardi, the famous football coach of the champion Green Bay Packer team, once told his team, "We will have a relentless pursuit of perfection." If a man can have that kind of vision for a game called football, then the servant of God can choose excellence. Being excellent is not about keeping up with others or with other churches, but being the best where you are. If you have a thousand dollar budget, you can't compete with another who has a budget of ten thousand or a million dollars. Be the best that you can be where you are. You are created in the image and likeness of God. *So God created man in His own image; in the image of God He created him, male and female He created them.* (See Genesis 1:27.) God is goal oriented.

🔑 When He starts talking to you about your destiny, He's got big plans.

He's got plans for the entire world. In order to reach the world, you must be excellent. If you're going to imitate God, you will have to be as excellent as He is. Dr. I.V. Hilliard said at a seminar Joselyn and I attended, "Average gets no attention so let's choose to be excellent." Romans 16:19 (NIV) *"but I want you to be wise about what is good, and innocent about what is evil."* Ephesians 5:1 sets the standard, *"Therefore be imitators of God as dear children."* How do you reach the goal and destiny in your heart? How does the servant get the harvest?

1. Determine what you want to give your life to and start today. Napoleon Hill said I can teach anyone how to get what they truly want in life. The problem is I can't find anybody who can tell me what they truly want. In 1 Timothy 4:13-16, Paul said to give attention to reading, exhorting or preaching, convincing others and teaching. That ought to keep us busy right there. Paul states in verse 15 to meditate on these things and give yourself entirely to them. I like what John Mason said, "Nothing significant was ever accomplished by a realistic person."

You ask, "How does the servant get the harvest?" By devoting ourselves entirely to it. Helen Keller said, "life is either a daring adventure or nothing...." What is it that you always wanted to do? If you want tomorrow to be different than today, you have to do something.

The harvest is waiting for the servant, but you must have a strategy to accomplish it. Take time to write down your personal mission for your life. Habakkuk 2:2-3 says,

> Then the Lord answered me and said: "Write the vision and make it plain on tablets, that he may run who reads it. For the vision is yet for an appointed time; but at the end it will speak, and it will not lie. Though it tarries, wait for it; because it will surely come, it will not tarry."

Have a plan, imagination, vision and hope. Write it down. For the harvest to be reachable, it must be readable. Write down where you want your life to go. Every trip should start with a map.

Several years ago, we wanted to go on a summer vacation. We decided to take three weeks and drive across the country. (Now, I don't advise this unless you have a bigger van than we did!) The first thing we did was to plan our stops. Then we called AAA and got a trip ticket. It showed us tourist information, where to find the hotels, fuel, and rest stops. There were some things we had to see others things not such a big deal. The Grand Canyon, Pikes Peak, Mississippi river those were big deals. So we planned ahead so we could take in the main sites. If we invested and planned for a three week vacation, how much more important is it for an entire life?

🔑 Have a plan. And understand that if you have one, you can adjust it at any time.

A few years ago, I read a study that I thought was very informative. The tests included people who were extremely successful, very successful, of average income and people who were on some kind of government assistance. Researchers asked them all the same questions. Do you have a plan for your life? Are you taking action on this plan? Did you write down your plan?

The results were fascinating. Three percent of the people polled said they had a plan, had written it down and were following it. Eleven percent said that they had a plan and were following it pretty closely. Fifty percent said they had a general idea, but only thought about it occasionally, while thirty-six percent gave no thought at all to their future. Of those polled, three percent were extremely wealthy, eleven percent were successful, fifty percent were barely getting along from week to week, and thirty-six percent were on some kind of government assistance—the exact same percentages. The difference between their financial situations wasn't educational or racial, ethnic or geographic. The only discernable difference the researchers could find between all these people was having a plan, writing it down and following it or not.

🔑 You are going to spend the rest of your life in your future.

You may as well plan it out. A wise servant must have a plan.

2. To reap the harvest, a servant must also be flexible to change his or her plans. Making adjustments is a lot easier than coming up with a new life plan every month. The first space missions and landings on the moon were filled with adjustments. On the first moon landing, Mission Control had to change course every ten minutes. Some corrections were minor, some were major, but they were made consistently. Be willing to adjust.

As the servant matures, superfluous things don't matter that much. The productive servant must be about His father's business as Jesus was in Luke 2:49. *"And He said to them, 'Why did you seek Me? Did you not know that I must be about My Father's business?"* I don't expect others who aren't about God's business to understand or agree with what's in my heart. Many unproductive Christians will try to talk you out of the will of God. There's an old saying, and it applies to them, "Misery loves company." And I've got news for you, the unproductive and the dysfunctional love company too. The servant can't afford to let the uncommitted affect his destiny. Unfortunately, I've had to let some old friends go who didn't want to follow God's plan for their lives. That doesn't mean I don't love them, or that I don't have anything at all to do with them. It means that those closest to us have to have the same heart. Ephesians 5:11 warns us, *"And have no fellowship with the unfruitful works of darkness, but rather expose them."*

The servant who wants to get the harvest must be excellent. Do your best to be your best. In the King James Version, of 2 Timothy 2:15 it says to study. Be prepared. We've all seen people who are unprepared and who try to just wing it. When you are unprepared, you're fooling no one but yourself.

You might say, "Danny, are you saying that you plan for every contingency?" Yes, as best I can, and I always ask God to help me be led by the Holy Spirit during my preparations. Excellence prepares for everything to go smoothly, but has a plan in place if it doesn't. Remember, there is thief. According to Romans 16:19-20, *"...but I want you to be wise in what is good, and simple concerning evil. And the God of peace will crush Satan under your feet shortly..."* In order to be excellent, find out what is good. I also know you want to be as productive as possible.

🔑 Productivity comes from a mindset and good work habits.

Commit to becoming a life long learner, so you can solve problems no matter where you are or what job you're doing. God designed you to solve problems others won't even notice. It's amazing how aptitude follows observation. Both the "how to" and the "what to do" are important. God can show you how to solve problems once you discover them. In life, people who solve problems always get rewarded. In Genesis 39:1-6, Joseph was taken to Egypt as a slave,

Now Joseph had been taken down to Egypt. And Potiphar, an officer of Pharaoh, captain of the guard, an Egyptian, bought him from the Ismaelites who had taken him down there. The Lord was with Joseph, and he was a successful man; and he was in the house of his master the Egyptian. And his master saw that the Lord was with him and that the Lord made all he did to prosper in his hand. So Joseph found favor in his sight, and served him. Then he made him overseer of his house, and all that he had he put under his authority. So it was, from the time that he had made him overseer of his house and all he had, that the Lord blessed the Egyptian's house for Joseph's sake; and the blessing of the Lord was on all that he had in the house and in the field. Thus he left all that he had in Joseph's hand, and he did not know what he had except for the bread he ate.

Let's look at just a few of Joseph's attributes.

1) He was a successful man.

2) The Lord was with him.

3) The Lord made all he did to prosper.

4) Joseph had the favor of the Lord.

5) Joseph served his master.

6) Joseph was made an overseer of all Potiphar had.

7) The blessing was on everything Joseph touched.

Joseph solved problems and was rewarded for it. In Genesis Chapter 40, Joseph finds himself wrongfully imprisoned after rebuffing the advances of Potiphar's wife. While he is there, Pharaoh's butler and baker, who are imprisoned as well, have strange dreams. Joseph solved the problem of interpreting the dreams, and the butler remembered it when Pharaoh himself had a troubling nightmare,

> *Then Pharaoh sent and called Joseph, and they brought him quickly out of the dungeon; and he shaved, changed his clothing, and came to Pharaoh. And Pharaoh said to Joseph, "I have had a dream, and there is no one who can interpret it. But I have heard it said of you that you can understand a dream, to interpret it."* (Genesis 41:14-15)

Once again, Joseph solved a problem, this time it was Pharaoh's dream and the interpretation of it. His problem solving abilities saved an entire nation.

🗝 Because of Joseph's ability and advice, he was rewarded.

> *So the advice was good in the eyes of Pharaoh and in the eyes of all his servants. And Pharaoh said to his servants, "Can we find such a one as this, a man in whom is the Spirit of God?" Then Pharaoh said to Joseph, 'Inasmuch as God has shown you all this, there is no one as discerning and wise as you. You shall be over my house, and all my people shall be ruled according to your word; only in regard to the throne will I be greater than you." And Pharaoh said to Joseph, "See, I have set you over all the land of Egypt." Then Pharaoh took his signet ring off his hand and put it on Joseph's hand; and he clothed him in garments of fine linen and put a gold chain around his neck. And he had him ride in the second*

*chariot which he had; and they cried out before him,
"Bow the knee!" So he set him over all the land of
Egypt. Pharaoh also said to Joseph, "I am Pharaoh,
and without your consent no man may lift his hand
or foot in all the land of Egypt." (Genesis 41:37-44)*

3. **To get a harvest, you must become a problem solver.**
If you allow the Word of God to develop within the good
ground of your heart, you will soon be a problem solver and
be rewarded in your own right. Proverbs 18:16 affirms it; *"A
man's gift makes room for him, and brings him before great
men."* Your gift will make room for you. The Lord wants
to lead all of us, but if you've not discovered the life within
the Word that's planted in the ground of a good heart, you'll
miss the greatest gift—knowing God.

4. **To get your harvest, you'll have to know God's voice.**
God wants to lead and speak to all His children. As a matter
of fact, He already has. John 10:27 tells us, *"My sheep hear
My voice, and I know them, and they follow Me."* His sheep
hear His voice, but do we distinguish it among all the chatter
in the world? God speaks to those who are glad to know,
glad to grow, and glad to go. Do you qualify? God led Abram
because he was glad to know, go and grow.

You too can be a problem solver, hear God's voice and
be rewarded. David solved the problem of Goliath, and
was rewarded with a wife and riches by Saul. Problems are
inevitable. You either solve them or ignore them. They either
define you or confine you. The armies of Israel hid from
Goliath. Instead of fixing the problem, they fled from it, and
David had to be the one to follow up.

5. **To get your harvest, you'll have to be above average.**
An average servant gets no attention. Average is the enemy of
your next level. God hasn't called any of His children to be
average. He hasn't called His children to barely get along and
experience joy once in a while. We've been called overcomers
in 1 John 5:4, *"For whatever is born of God overcomes the*

world. And this is the victory that has overcome the world–our faith." We've been called the head and not the tail, above and not beneath in Deuteronomy 28:13:

> "*And the Lord will make you the head and not the tail; you shall be above only, and not be beneath, if you heed the commandments of the Lord your God, which I command you today, and are careful to observe them.*"

You've also been called blessed according to Deuteronomy 28:1-6.

Our God is awesome, and we should show forth His praise to a lost world. Servants of the King should be different because we have hope. I know salvation has changed me and my expectations in life.

⚿ Average people rarely leave a mark in this life, and don't reach their God given destiny.

I know that's a strong statement, but it's true. You must have passion and be determined to overcome obstacles. There is resistance at every threshold of opportunity. Be a person that rises above average and pushes through resistance. Servants of God understand that the righteous have to take new ground for the Kingdom by force. Matthew 11:12 reads, "*And from the days of John the Baptist until now, the Kingdom of Heaven suffers violence, and the violent take it by force.*"

6. To get your harvest, you must develop diligence.

⚿ The diligent servant distinguishes between what will be productive, and what is just activity.

Being busy doesn't always translate into progress. Haven't we all met people who were always running? Busy, busy, busy! But does all that busyness translate into productivity? Focused servants know what works. It's hard to hang around people who are unable to make decisions. I'm not the most patient person in the world, and one thing that really gets me going is dealing with indecisive people. I'm not real big on fast food, but the menus haven't changed much in fifteen years. If you're at a counter, it shouldn't take you fifteen minutes to decide what you want. We're not average people. We're filled with wisdom and purpose. We should be able to make a decision between a burger and chicken.

It's hard to make a sharp decision with dull thinking. Servants know what to do, and they know if what they're doing is going to produce. I don't get excited by staff meetings at the office or by counseling sessions. It's not that I see them as unimportant. It's just not a part of my natural gifting. My best counseling is done from the pulpit when I preach. My best leadership happens while the staff is working on projects, and I am teaching along the way. Meetings are just not my strength, so most times I try and stay out of the way, rather than cause a distraction. I like the creative aspect of church work: new ministries, structures or outreaches. But the nuts and bolts I leave to the experts who enjoy the day-to-day.

A servant that will be productive, not only knows his own strengths, but knows the strengths of the people who work with him. Each of us has strengths and weaknesses. I study people to discover their passions. I know that if you make a connection to a person with passion, you'll get production. Furthering the Kingdom of God is what this is all about. Winning the lost, teaching the young, training new leaders and empowering them to fulfill their destiny, is productive for Him. I steer clear of people without passion. I want to associate with people who have a history, who have lifelong friends and who get along well with others. I have made mistakes a few times when I ignored my instincts regarding people without long term relationships. I want people in my life and organization, who can last over the long haul.

Servants understand that growing good seed in good ground has the potential to maximize their lives. They can become the champions they have dreamed of becoming. If you're ever going to optimize your potential in life, there are keys you'll have to implement.

1. **Organize your life around what is most important.** What do you want to accomplish?

🔑 Be focused and really think.

Most people won't think for themselves. They allow others to define their successes for them. At one time, I thought that if I had a million dollars, that would be success. That's not success, that's an amount. I won't let others define my borders. You can easily attain a million dollars if you focus. For Joselyn and I, that mark was just several real estate deals. Then I had to come up with a new boundary. You can have all the money and all the toys, but if you don't have peace and joy, you don't have much. I don't want to get to the end of life and ministry and find that I've lost what's most dear to me which are, family, friends, memories, and most importantly, my relationship with God. Focus on what's important, and money will follow. If teaching fulfills you, then go for it! You may never get rich teaching. You may have to offset your income by writing books or lecturing. But find out what fulfills you and go for it!

2. **Keep your body and your mind healthy.** It's amazing how people abuse themselves and sacrifice their health for success.

🔑 Burning the candle at both ends gets you burned out twice as fast.

We have a dear lady in our church who is awesome in every way. She's happily married and owns her own international business with hundreds of employees. Currently, she's struggling with some health issues. I can say that she is one of the most courageous people I have ever met in my life. One day she told Joselyn and me that the sickness she struggles with today came as a result of trying to build her business. The long hours, the late nights, stresses beyond the normal, coupled with dealing with employees, the bottom line and international concerns, took their toll on her health. She is so strong, but we can all learn from her that we need to take care of our minds and our bodies.

I do my best to keep the drama level down. I don't let toxic people have much of my time and attention. Philippians 4:4-9 tells us to think on the good things.

3. Simplify everything. I believe in the K.I.S.S. principle. Keep it simple saints. (Which, incidentally, is the title of my next book.) Streamline, eliminate and cancel the unnecessary as soon as you can. I was scheduled to have a meeting with some local businessmen recently. I was speaking to one of them who I had met in my travels during the day. He asked if we were still meeting. I said why don't we meet right now and not put it off and tie up another day. In five minutes, we cleared up our meeting, he called the other businessman and we saved another afternoon by just handling it then. I don't believe in meeting for the sake of meetings. I found that much of what I was doing, I did because of tradition. There's the old story about a young couple who had just gotten back from their honeymoon. The new bride was planning to cook their first meal as a married couple. As she's preparing the pot roast, her husband walks in as she cuts off the end of the roast and places it in the pan. "Why did you cut off the end of the roast, dear?" "I don't know," she answered. "That's just how Mom taught me." "Curious," her husband said, "Would you call her and ask her why she taught you to do that?" So the bride called her mother and mom answered her, "Well, I don't know. That's just how my mom taught me." They laugh and say, "Well, let's call grandma and find out!" Mom calls grandma and asks, "Mom, why did you teach us to cut off the end of the pot roast and put it into the pan?" Grandma says, "Because I had a small pan."

Simplify your life, your business, and your ministry. You'll enjoy it more. Whether you have a house full of kids or you're at the office with employees or co-workers, create an atmosphere of simplicity and order.

4. Understand human nature. They say that there are three types of people in the world. Those who make things happen, those who watch things happen, and those who wonder what happened. Human nature is so predictable. Paul writes in 1 Thessalonians 5:12, *"And I urge you, brethren, to recognize those who labor among you, and are over you in the Lord and admonish you."* Know those who are around you, and if you are in a position of influence, steer people to positions in which they can soar.

We all have met chronically unhappy people and I trust that you have as few of them as possible around you. People are always the solution, and they are always the problem, too. I don't know many ways to have a fulfilled life without having human contact. So learn about different personality types and how to work with them. You can get pretty jaded in life and not trust anyone, but you won't get much accomplished alone. Team work is rewarding. There's an acronym for team: Together Each Accomplishes More. It doesn't get much better than a staff meeting where people are really involved creatively and progress is made. It's a great feeling of camaraderie and productivity. Get to know human nature, and put people in a position to win.

5. Follow someone who has been there and done that. You're never such a big shot that you can't follow someone who has already been there before you. My pastor has seen almost everything in his forty five years of ministry. He and his wife not only have experience, but a discerning spirit. I've been able to tap into that on many occasions. Contrary to popular belief, experience is not the best teacher. Someone else's experience is better. There's no virtue in hitting yourself on the thumb with a hammer the second time. If you're a pastor, go to conferences of church builders. Learn from those who have already been there. Buy books and teaching series that can help you get to your next level.

6. Develop the attitude of gratitude. Be thankful. The following Scripture tell us to praise God for our successes, *"Oh, give thanks to the Lord, for He is good! For His mercy endures forever."* (Psalm 118:1)

To optimize our potential, we must be thankful, gracious people. I've never met an unappreciative person who is happy. I attempt to thank people for coming to church each service, because there are more than two hundred churches in our community where these same folks could attend, and I'm glad that they chose ours. Notes, cards and calls are always a great way to show you really care.

7. To optimize your potential, be a giver. Luke 6:38 tells us, *"Give and it shall be given unto you, pressed down, shaken together, and running over will be put into your bosom."* This is true not just of money, which is obvious in this passage, but of your time and talent. Marriages and relationships can be very tough, and they need consistent maintenance. God may use you to give of your time and experience to help some young couple see things with a different perspective. Give of your time and experience.

The servant wants to optimize every opportunity for growth and development. They especially want to help others reach their potential.

Chapter 14
Conclusion

According to Jesus, the way the world works is very simple. It's so simple that we should listen to His words. It's so simple that your mind will want to complicate it. If God wanted to keep knowledge from us, He would never have explained it so many times or given us illustrations to help us understand. The truth is hidden for us not from us. Mark 4:11-12, *"And He said unto them, 'Unto you it is given to know the mystery of the Kingdom of God."* At the end of vs. 12, the translators used the phrase *"their sins should be forgiven them."* The 'sin' to which Jesus refers is the willful rejection of the truth. Mark 4:12 (Amplified Version),

> *"In order that they may [indeed] look and look but not see and perceive, and may hear and hear but not grasp and comprehend, lest haply they should turn again, and it [their willful rejection of the truth] should be forgiven them."*

So those that are outside, meaning the legalistic and the unconverted, are those who are willfully rejecting the truth.

Today, there are Bibles everywhere. The Bible is the number one best seller of all time. In fact, it's the number one selling book every month, but the media doesn't report it that way. Millions are in print, and millions more are sold every year. In this country, we have Christian bookstores, and churches in every city and town. We have Christian radio and TV broadcasts flooding the airwaves. (And now, we have bloggers and websites reaching out with the Word over the internet and covering the world through Facebook and Twitter.) Yet there remain those who are unconverted, those who are willfully rejecting the truth.

It is just as true today as it was in Jesus' day; people are willfully rejecting the truth and replacing it with cheap substitutes. Today's generation, at least those of us who live in the civilized world, will have no excuses.

People replace the truth of the power of God, which lives in each person's heart, with myths, wives' tales, and scientific mumbo jumbo; all of which are easily debunked. These theories and myths are as silly as a blind man looking for a black cat in a dark room that's not there. Evolution cannot be proven. The giraffe proves that. Its heart is extremely powerful to have it pump blood all the way up the neck. If God didn't put a valve to regulate the blood pressure it would blow the top of its head off each time it lowered its head to take a drink of water. You mean evolution got all these intricate details synched up right with the first two giraffes? Now that takes a lot of faith to believe. Albert Einstein said, "If the facts don't fit the theory, change the facts." He also said, "I want to know all God's thoughts; all the rest are just details." My Bible School President, Kenneth E. Hagin, would periodically say, "Some people are educated beyond their intellect." Scientists, with all their assets, education and resources, still cannot prove their theory of evolution, the Big Bang, or cosmic coincidence. People willfully reject God's truth. They make a conscious decision to believe that all those parables and principles that Jesus left are just stories.

Jesus taught us that Kingdom keys work like a sower sowing seed in different conditions of soil. He explains these verses more fully in Mark 4:13-23:

Then in (verses 21-23), Jesus teaches to us the obvious uses of a lamp or light, *"Also He said to them, 'Is a lamp brought to be put under a basket or under a bed? Is it not to be set on a lamp stand?"*

You don't take a lamp or a candle and put it under a basket or bed. If you do, you can't benefit from the light. You maximize a candle by putting it in a holder on a stand so that it can dispel the darkness. The light of the Word needs to be planted in the good ground of your heart so that you can maximize its benefits. Enshrining the Bible and never opening it doesn't maximize its light and power, reading it and meditating on it does. And you plant it by reading, studying, and speaking the Word. The Bible makes this plain over and over again. The enemy's plan is to stop you from making the Word of God priority in your life. If this happens, things can never change. And that's The Key in a nutshell. Life and power are in the Word.

What you get out of the Bible isn't up to God. It's up to you! The Scripture teaches us that the measure you use will be measured back to you (See Matthew 7:2.). The priority you place on the Word of God (Mark 4:24 Amplified) determines the power that's measured back. If you plant the Word in the good ground in your heart, more Word and life will be added to you. But if you have no Word and no priority and conviction for it, whatever you do have will be taken away by the devil. Jesus even said it in Mark 4:15, *"When they hear, Satan comes immediately and takes away the Word that was sown in their hearts."*

Just because you believe today, and you are following Christ today, is no indication that you will be in five years. I know lots of people who I went to Bible school with, that aren't serving God today. Why? Because they stopped hearing and doing the Word of God. The key is that there's life in the Word and you have to keep putting it into your heart.

The Bible teaches another key that unlocks the rest of the parables.

🔑 The harvest comes progressively.

You don't sow a seed one day and the next day; expect to eat the tomato or watermelon. Growing a crop takes a season. There's a process that has to take place.

You and I can only plan for the predictable process of a seed; planting, growing and harvest. If you need instant help or a miracle, God is certainly still in that business.

As my pastor says, "God still has the recipe for manna in the wilderness." But, miracles always border on catastrophe. Miracles are out of our control. If you want to live beyond just enough, live beyond catastrophe, then seed time and harvest is predicable, dependable and is in your control. (See Galatians 6:7 and (Luke 6:38.)

Most of the time, growth takes place in your life below the ground, where the roots are. The roots represent maturity and stability, and they support the growth above the ground, which everybody sees. You may see your pastor or favorite TV preacher and think, 'Wow, look at the tree or the fruit!" What you really should be amazed about, are the roots. If you see people who are successful in God's Kingdom, one thing is for certain, they have spent time alone in private, developing a root system that no one else can see. To maintain the structural integrity of a skyscraper, you must have a foundation. It's the same with your spiritual life. We have all seen very talented and charismatic people with tremendous ability rise to the top of their professions crash and burn. Not because they don't have the gifts and ambition to get to the top, but because they didn't have the character and foundation to keep them there. There is a root problem. The plant needs time to grow properly. The parable of the mustard seed teaches us that, although the seed is small and seemingly insignificant, if it remains planted, it can grow and help support the life and future of others.

Don't get frustrated if you start small. Everyone does. The only person that starts at the top is a grave digger. Everyone else starts the process one step at a time. Be patient, and you'll see things develop. And remember, you never learned anything in school that you weren't tested on.

Jesus gave the disciples the Word: *"Let us cross over to the other side."* (Luke 8:22) According to the Bible, Satan will come to steal the Word when you hear it. We see this lived out in the disciples' reactions. Jesus gave them the Word.

The question is what type of soil did the seed of the Word get planted into? Was their root system developed? What priority did they place on what Jesus had said? What were the disciples expecting to receive? These questions are a vital part of the outcome. Jesus didn't say, 'Let's start crossing over to the other side, get halfway across, get caught in a storm and drown.' That's not what He said at all!

But the circumstances were contrary to a safe arrival on the other shore. The disciples looked at the circumstances long enough that the things they saw affected their expectations. In fact, it affected them so much that they woke Jesus to ask Him, "Teacher, do you not care that we are perishing?" We get a promise, we pray and believe, and then Satan causes circumstances to be contrary to what the Lord said. We have a choice. Do we believe Him? "Let us cross over to the other side?" Or do we give in to our senses and emotions, and reason away the power of God's Word? In verses 39-41, Jesus spoke the Word and challenged the disciples by telling them, 'Why didn't you speak your faith, even in the middle of the storm?'

The good news is, with Jesus, if you fail the test once, there will be another chance to pass it coming along soon.

Andrew Wammack shared this great illustration. Do you remember High School science class? Most of us can remember the illustration that used 2 one gallon tin gasoline cans, each of which was heated by a Bunsen burner. One can was empty, and one had water in it. Once the cans had been heated for a little while, the flame was turned off, and lids were put on each can. Something very interesting happened next. The empty one gallon can began to cool, and as it did, it collapsed in on itself and crumbled. Meanwhile, the other can, which was full of water, just cooled off without any structural damage. The one which was supported by something inside it withstood the pressure of heating and cooling. While the one that was empty bent and crumbled.

It was crushed by the pressure of the changing temperature of the air.

That's a lot like us, isn't it? When life's heat and pressure comes, if you're empty inside, you rarely make it through the trial. But if you're full inside, you'll be standing long after the heat cools. Life is filled with circumstances that can either bend or break you. Or you can let the heat temper you and make you stronger. It's what is in you that will make the difference. (See Mark 4:23.) Keep the Word and you'll be good ground.

The most important thing, The Key, is how's your heart? Are you good ground for your seed? Will you produce even in the harshest of circumstances? Will you keep hearing the Word even though the process is taking longer than you thought it would? Will you be the one that produces? It's a choice. God's no respecter of persons; He's a respecter of faith. The Bible makes it clear that there is a decision of faith that must be made, *"Then Peter opened his mouth and said, 'In truth I perceive that God shows no partiality.'"* (Acts 10:34)

In Matthew 25, the parable of the 10 virgins is introduced. Five virgins had the wicks of their lamps trimmed and carried oil to fuel them, while the five without oil weren't prepared for any contingencies. If you're filled and ready, you won't be crushed by the pressure of waiting in dark times. If you're not prepared, the weight and pressure of life's circumstances are designed to crush you. Ephesians 5:18 tell us, *"And do not be drunk with wine, in which is dissipation; but be filled with the Spirit."* Paul is teaching us to always be filled with the Spirit. In the Amplified Bible this Scripture reads, *"And do not get drunk with wine, for that is debauchery; but ever be filled and stimulated with the [Holy] Spirit."* Paul tells us this is a continual filling. You can stay filled so you won't be crushed.

The Christian life is supposed to be a victorious life. Its

work, but you win. Just like anything else, you must maintain your vigilance and confidence in God, because you have an adversary.

🔑 Knowing who you are in Christ, and what your rights and privileges are, will keep the thief from encroaching on what belongs to you by covenant.

Know that you are a new creation in Him. *"Therefore, if anyone is in Christ, he is a new creation; old things have passed away; behold, all things have become new."* (2 Corinthians 5:17)

As a believer, you're made righteous at the new birth. (See 2 Corinthians 5:21.) You're not becoming the righteousness of God, you were made righteous. So if you're not filled continually and mindful of this fact, the devil will try to beat your brains in with condemnation each and every time you sin. When I sin, it's between me and God. I go to the person I sinned against and repent, and I go to God and repent. 1 John 1:9 tells us how to approach God: *"If we confess our sins, He is faithful and just to forgive us our sins and to cleanse us from all unrighteousness."* Repent literally means to turn around and go the other way. Since Jesus has paid the price for all sin, turn the other way when you discover you've missed it.

Satan has no part in it. Jesus has already taken our sin for us. *"There is therefore now no condemnation to those who are in Christ Jesus, who do not walk according to the flesh, but according to the Spirit."* (Romans 8:1) I won't let the enemy encroach on my righteousness, because it belongs to me.

🔑 The battlefield is your mind. It must be dominated and controlled by what God has said so that the devil can't control you.

Worry will try to control your mind. Fear will try to

control your mind. The unknown and fear of the future will try to stop you. How do you combat fear, anxiety and worry? The Word of God tells you what you should be filled with:

1. You should be filled with all the fullness of God. *"...to know the love of Christ which passes knowledge; that you may be filled with all the fullness of God."* (Ephesians 3:19)

2. You should be filled with the knowledge of His will. *"For this reason we also, since the day we heard it, do not cease to pray for you, and to ask that you may be filled with the knowledge of His will in all wisdom and spiritual understanding."* (Colossians 1:9)

3. You should be filled with joy. *"Rejoice in the Lord, always, again I say rejoice."* (Philippians 4:4)

Of course, dealing with our thoughts is a full time job. Jesus knew it, and He told us what to do. We should be as smart as the birds and the flowers. God takes care of them without worry on their part, and we should trust Him for the same.

Fear comes with torment. God hasn't called any of us to torture ourselves with anxiety. We have an all powerful God who can be trusted. These Scriptures tell us so:

"Trust in the Lord with all your heart; and lean not unto your own understanding; in all your ways acknowledge Him, and He shall direct your paths." (Proverbs 3:5-6)

"Therefore humble yourselves under the mighty hand of God, that He may exalt you in due time, casting all your care upon Him, for He cares for you." (1 Peter 5:6-7)

You can do this. Each time worry and fear knock at your door, you can answer with faith, and they will flee. Negative thoughts must be dealt with. They must be challenged with what God said.

🔑 The Final Key
Continually hear the Word
(Mark 4:23)

By controlling your thought life and continually renewing your mind, you are cultivating good ground in your heart. The power to transform our minds and hearts is supernaturally built into the Word. *"The law of the Lord is perfect converting the soul."* (Psalm 19:7)

It may be hard for you to see, but as you're putting the Word of God in your mind and heart, development is taking place. Every moment you think good thoughts you're taking back lost ground. Today's a brand new day. Just like gravity or the current in a river, your thoughts are continually working for you or against you. You are either creating function or dysfunction. Eve used her thoughts in a wrong way. Then these thoughts created a desire for the fruit. Thoughts are active and always in motion. They are creating something all the time.

Eve kept looking at the fruit and she was deceived first in her mind. Then the action came. She could envision herself eating and being as smart as God. (See Genesis 3:1-7.) As you think in your heart so are you. It all started with a question and deception from the serpent but could have been stopped by proactive thinking on Eve's part. She should have asked herself the question, "What did God say?" It's the same with the Word in your heart. The key to the Parable of the Sower is working for you as you renew your mind. The hard heart, the stones, and the thorns will gradually leave, and good ground will replace it. You should eliminate anything that competes with the seeds' ability to produce. Negative words, thoughts or distractions have to be stopped so progress can be made. Power and life are in the seed, and that seed is the Word of God. You till the ground, and you plant. You water the seed by study and prayer and meditating on it. You wait a period of time, and you get the crop.

And that's how the world works according to Jesus.

Walt Disney World in Orlando, Florida is our family's favorite vacation and study spot. Although I studied many hours for this book, the bulk of it was written on Disney World property. So from the place that has brought us years of memories and has inspired creativity, I trust *Keys to Maximizing Your Harvest: Parable of the Sower* will bless you and inspire you to keep on hearing.

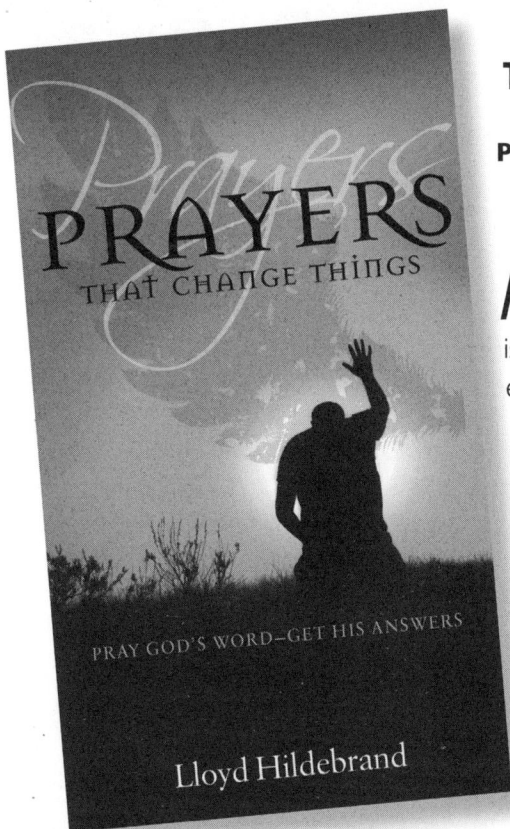

Prayers That Change Things
Pray God's Word— Get His Answers
by Lloyd Hildebrand

Prayers That Change Things is a new book by an established writer of books on prayer, Lloyd·B. Hildebrand, who co-authored the very popular *Prayers That Prevail* series, *Bible Prayers for All Your Needs*, *Praying the Psalms*, *Healing Prayers*, and several others. This new book contains prayers about personal feelings and situations, prayers that are built directly from the Bible. The reader will discover that praying the Scriptures will truly bring about changes to so many things, especially their outlook on life and the circumstances of life. These life-imparting, life-generating, life-giving, and life-sustaining prayers are sure to bring God's answers to meet the believer's needs. Pray them from your heart; then wait for God to speak to you. Remember, He always speaks through His Word.

This revolutionary approach joins the power of prayer with the power of God's Word.

ISBN: 978-1-61036-105-7
MM / 192 pages

"The Consummate Apologetics Bible...
Everything you ever need to share your faith."

"The Evidence Bible is the reservoir overflowing with everything evangelistic—powerful quotes from famous people, amazing anecdotes, sobering last words, informative charts, and a wealth of irrefutable evidence to equip, encourage, and enlighten you, like nothing else.

I couldn't recommend it more highly."

– Kirk Cameron

Compiled by Ray Comfort

This edition of *The Evidence Bible* includes notes, commentaries, and quotations that make it a comprehensive work of apologetics and evangelism that will be helpful to every believer. It covers a variety of practical topics, including the following:

- How to answer objections to Christianity
- How to talk about Christ with people of other religions
- How to counter evolutionary theories, while providing evidence for God's creation
- How to grow in Christ
- How to use the Ten Commandments when witnessing

There is no other Bible like this one. Every soul-winner who wants to lead others to Christ will want a copy of *The Evidence Bible*, because it provides springboards for preaching and witnessing, shares insights from well-known Christian leaders, gives points for open-air preaching, reveals the scientific facts contained within the Bible, and supplies the believer with helpful keys to sharing one's faith. The Bible is "the sword of the Spirit," and this edition of the Bible will motivate believers to become true spiritual warriors in their daily interactions with others.

THE
EVIDENCE
BIBLE NKJV

All You Need to Understand and Defend Your Faith

COMMENTARY BY
RAY COMFORT

ISBN: 9780882705255
PB

*Also available in
duo tone leather.*

ISBN: 9780882708973

The
Evidence
Bible

Irrefutable
evidence
for the
thinking mind

King James Version
New Testament,
Psalms and
Proverbs

Compiled by
Ray Comfort

Prove God's existence.

Answer 100 common objections to Christianity.

Show the Bible's supernatural origin.

Bridge Logos

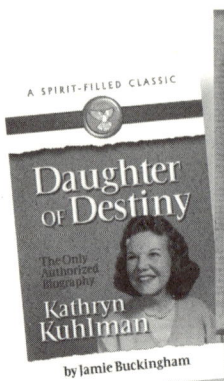

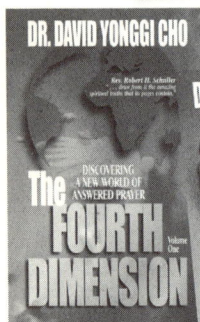

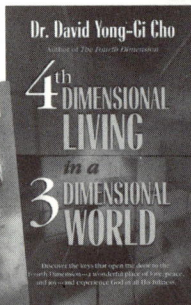

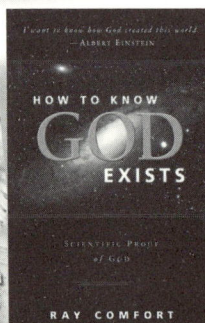

Top 20

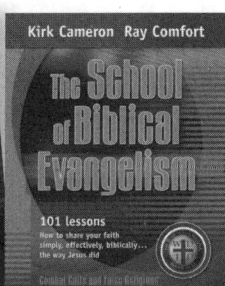

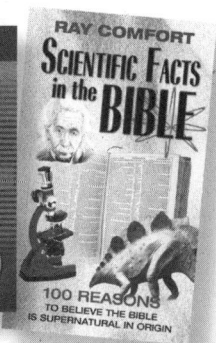

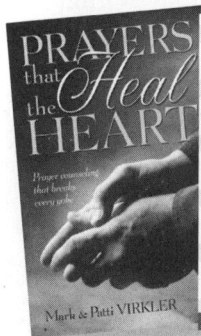

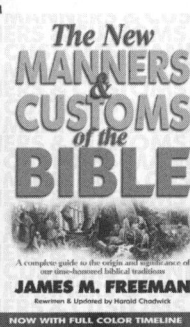

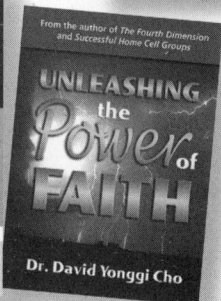

Pure Gold Classics
Timeless Truth in a Distinctive, Best-Selling Collection

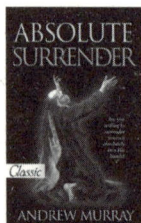

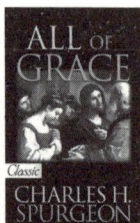

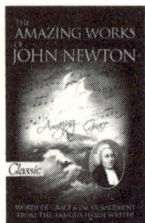

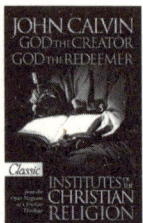

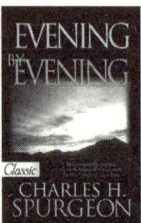

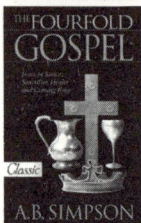

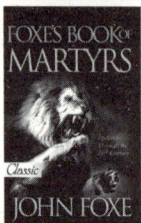

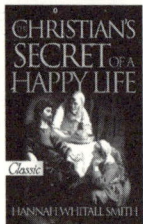

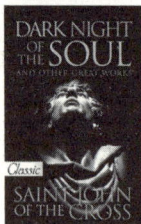

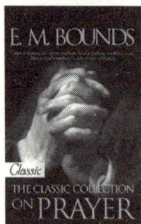

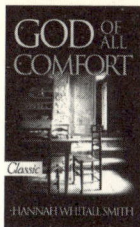
GOD OF ALL COMFORT — HANNAH WHITALL SMITH

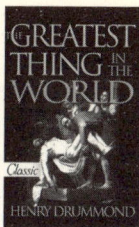
THE GREATEST THING IN THE WORLD — HENRY DRUMMOND

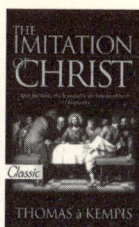
THE IMITATION OF CHRIST — THOMAS à KEMPIS

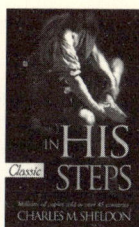
IN HIS STEPS — CHARLES M. SHELDON

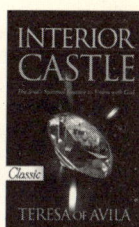
INTERIOR CASTLE — TERESA OF AVILA

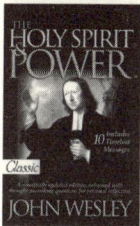
THE HOLY SPIRIT POWER — JOHN WESLEY

R. A. TORREY — THE HOLY SPIRIT WHO HE IS AND WHAT HE DOES

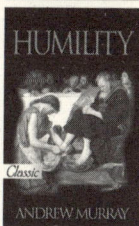
HUMILITY — ANDREW MURRAY

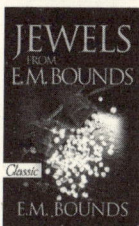
JEWELS FROM E. M. BOUNDS — E. M. BOUNDS

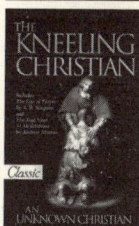
THE KNEELING CHRISTIAN — AN UNKNOWN CHRISTIAN

MADAME JEANNE GUYON

MORNING BY MORNING — CHARLES H. SPURGEON

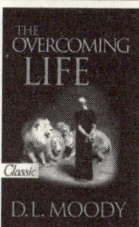
THE OVERCOMING LIFE — D. L. MOODY

THE PILGRIM'S PROGRESS IN MODERN ENGLISH — JOHN BUNYAN

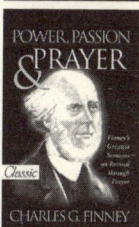
POWER, PASSION & PRAYER — CHARLES G. FINNEY

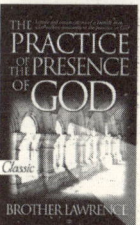
THE PRACTICE OF THE PRESENCE OF GOD — BROTHER LAWRENCE

SECRET POWER — D. L. MOODY

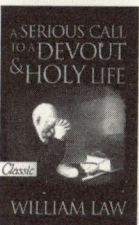
A SERIOUS CALL TO A DEVOUT & HOLY LIFE — WILLIAM LAW

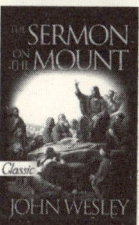
THE SERMON ON THE MOUNT — JOHN WESLEY

SINNERS IN THE HANDS OF AN ANGRY GOD — JONATHAN EDWARDS

THE SOVEREIGNTY OF GOD — A. W. PINK

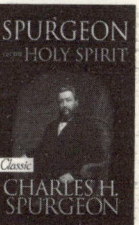
SPURGEON ON THE HOLY SPIRIT — CHARLES H. SPURGEON

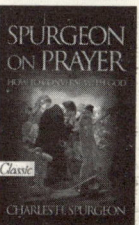
SPURGEON ON PRAYER — CHARLES H. SPURGEON

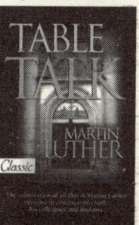
TABLE TALK — MARTIN LUTHER

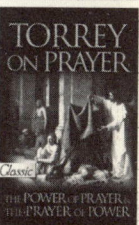
TORREY ON PRAYER — THE POWER OF PRAYER AND THE PRAYER OF POWER

TOZER — FELLOWSHIP OF THE BURNING HEART

TOZER: MYSTERY OF THE HOLY SPIRIT — A. W. TOZER

WALKING WITH GOD — THE ANDREW MURRAY TRILOGY ON SANCTIFICATION

WILLIAM WILBERFORCE — GREATEST WORKS

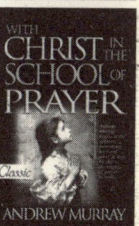
WITH CHRIST IN THE SCHOOL OF PRAYER — ANDREW MURRAY